TAKE THE PLACE'S
FINGERPRINT.
Forget words such as
resource, site, customers
and public. Abstractions
lead us astray.
Think and talk about
PLACES AND
PEOPLE.

Get to know your
GHOSTS.
The hidden and unseen
STORIES
AND
LEGENDS
are as important
as the visible.

GROUND
YOURSELF,
attachment is the
first step to
CHANGING
THE WORLD.

Don't fossilise places.
HISTORY
is a continuing process,
not just the past.
Celebrate time, place
and the seasons with
FEASTS AND
FESTIVALS.

Work for
LOCAL
IDENTITY

and automatic ordering
from pattern books
*which homogenise
and deplete.*

Our **imagination** needs
DIVERSITY
and variegation.
WE NEED
STANDARDS,
*not
standardisation.*

JETTISON YOUR CAR
whenever you can and go
by public transport.
PLACES ARE FOR
PEOPLE
AND
NATURE.
*Cars detach us from places
and unwittingly cause
their destruction.*

KNOW YOUR
PLACE.
rts and surveys are
ot the same as
NOWLEDGE
AND
ISDOM.
*expertise needs to
meet with aboriginal,
place-based knowledge so
that we can make the*
BEST OF BOTH
WORLDS.

THE **LAND** IS
SACRED
in many cultures. Why
have we put a protective
noose around the
SPECTACULAR
AND THE
SPECIAL
and left the rest?
*All of our surroundings are
important to someone.*

Buy things that are
LOCALLY
DISTINCTIVE
AND
LOCALLY
MADE
*– such as food and souvenirs.
Resist the things that can be
found anywhere.*

JOURNEYS THROUGH
ENGLAND IN PARTICULAR:
Coasting

JOURNEYS THROUGH

ENGLAND IN PARTICULAR:

Coasting

SUE CLIFFORD & ANGELA KING

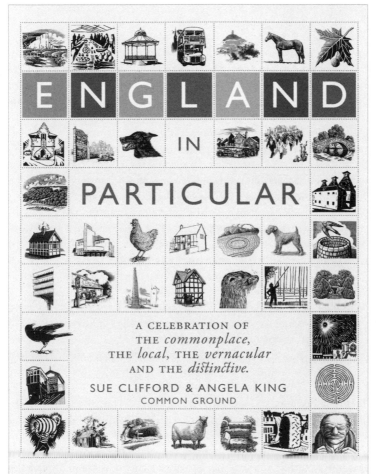

ENGLAND

IN

PARTICULAR

A CELEBRATION OF
THE *commonplace*,
THE *local*, THE *vernacular*
AND THE *distinctive*.

SUE CLIFFORD & ANGELA KING
COMMON GROUND

Acclaim for *England in Particular*

'A living portrait of England here and now, with all the narrative and mystery of the past attached ... The book is gracefully written, phenomenally knowledgeable, and simply exhilarating, speaking as it does of the extraordinary things that are all around us, if we are only prepared to open our eyes to them.'   FAY WELDON

'There is an impressive synoptic quality to the essays, which are given further unity by the lyrical character of the prose, by the rich, warm, humorous, celebratory tone throughout and the lightness of the authors' touch with the facts. Yet this is also a wonderfully scholarly book ... The book is an absolute delight for dippers, but there is a serious and unifying philosophy underpinning it ... The abiding satisfaction of this superb book is to make us aware, perhaps for the first time, of something as wonderful and simple as a hollow way, and to allow us to appreciate it as both rural commonplace and national treasure all at once.'

MARK COCKER, *Guardian*

'This book is, if you like, a sermon on the art of cherishing, and also on the art of noticing. It is not a question of clinging to the past; rather of accepting that the past is what gives us definition and existence.'

SIMON BARNES, *The Times*

England in Particular was No 4 in *The Times* Top Ten Books of 2006.

'It should be added to Dorothy Hartley's similarly inspiring book published in 1954 called *Food in England*, to Richard Mabey's *Flora Britannica* and the equally wonderful *Birds Britannica*, to make a quartet of books guaranteed to receive enthusiasm for our island home. This book is the antidote to surfing the net. Spend an afternoon in its company and the view from your window will never be the same again.'

SIMONE SEKERS, *Blackmore Vale Magazine*

'This book is not a description but a manifesto, not a catalogue of charms but an urge to action and to a new way of seeing England. It is a ragbag of riches dragged up from all over England into which you can plunge your hand, elbow- and shoulder-deep. Here, the authors say over and over again, are the valuable things which you had scarcely noticed were valuable before. As a result, it is a deeply optimistic book. Gravestones matter as much as graffiti, grassy triangles and granite: all take their place as part of the language that the English use to know who they are.'

ADAM NICOLSON, *Evening Standard*

'An entrancing green alphabet ... "The land is our most elaborate story board," say Sue Clifford and Angela King as they demonstrate this truth in seemingly countless small essays, each one a brief masterpiece of combined natural and social history ... this is a book for all English seasons and for every English mile.'   RONALD BLYTHE

'This wise and witty and broad-shouldered celebration is the triumphant fruition of their work with Common Ground.'   RICHARD MABEY

'Thank heavens for this book. *England in Particular* does everything that the ideal grandmother would, with equal charm and perhaps an even greater depth of accuracy and information. It should become part of every well-organised family.'   CLIVE ASLET, *Country Life*

'As vital as it is joyous, and as timely as it is inspired ... It should join Shakespeare and the Bible as a "must have" on any English man or woman's desert island.'   HUGH FEARNLEY-WHITTINGSTALL

'It should be at every curious Englishman's bedside.'

ALAN TITCHMARSH

CONTENTS

CELEBRATING LOCAL DISTINCTIVENESS

This book is about the extraordinary richness of our everyday surroundings; the landscapes, buildings, people and wildlife that give meaning to the places we know.

It is about the commonplace; for us to value it, a creature does not have to be endangered, a building does not have to be monumental, a prospect does not have to be breathtaking. A place may not even be 'ours' for us to feel attached to it. We just need to know something of it; it has to mean something to us.

Everywhere is somewhere. What makes each place unique is the conspiracy of nature and culture; the accumulation of story upon history upon natural history.

At Common Ground we forged the idea of *local distinctiveness* to embody this concept. It is a dynamic thing, constantly evolving as places change – it is not about preserving the status quo, creating a frozen moment – and it includes the invisible as well as the visible: symbols, festivals and legends stand alongside hedgerows, hills and houses.

We have focused on aspects of locality – archaeology, architecture, landscape, language, food, folklore, events, engineering – that interact with one another at the level of the street, the neighbourhood, the parish.

Why England? Because we know it best. But we offer a way of looking that has universal potential, though it is best done on an intimate scale.

Why A to Z? The alphabet helps us to break some conventions; it liberates us from classifying things, from following history as an arrow through time, from organising hierarchies. It shuffles and juxtaposes in ways that surprise. This can change what we see, make things we take for granted seem new to us; it may encourage us into action. We hope this book helps you to look at your own place, to see it through new eyes, to cherish it and to take it into your own hands.

SUE CLIFFORD & ANGELA KING

Notes

England in Particular: a celebration of the commonplace, local, the vernacular and the distinctive. Sue Clifford & Angela King. Hodder & Stoughton 2006. Saltyard 2013. The original book is over 500 pages long with nearly 600 essays. It has a substantial preliminary essay, a fuller biography and an index.

The essays and illustrations in this new series are all taken from this book.

Journeys Through England in Particular: Coasting

Journeys Through England in Particular: On Foot

The English Counties

The Historic Counties are used. We have done our best to follow the bounds laid down a thousand years ago or more, helped by old maps and gazetteers, especially that online, produced by the Association of British Counties. Inevitably we have found it difficult and admit to inconsistencies especially in and around the cities.

'What do you consider the largest map that would be really useful?'

'About six inches to the mile.'

'Only six inches!' exclaimed Mein Herr. 'We very soon got to six yards to the mile. Then we tried a hundred yards to the mile. And then came the grandest idea of all! We actually made a map of the country, on the scale of a mile to the mile!'

'Have you used it much?' I enquired.

'It has never been spread out yet,' said Mein Herr: 'the farmers objected: they said it would cover the whole country, and shut out the sunlight! So we now use the country itself, as its own map, and I assure you it does nearly as well.'

LEWIS CARROLL, from *Sylvie and Bruno Concluded*

ALBION

This elusive old name for Britain may derive from *albus*, Latin for white. Many commentators mention this through time and it is both plausible and beguiling. This island is bounded to the south by high chalk cliffs kept constantly bright and white by rockfalls into the sea, and coasting seafarers making their way from the Mediterranean would easily recognise it from the description.

Others make Celtic claim – Albio, Alba or Alban(y), a name for all the islands of Great Britain or of parts of it (Scotland is sometimes cast as Alban).

One clutch of explanations has the giant Albion, son of Poseidon/ Neptune, ruling the land for 44 years followed by his giant sons. Given that one old name for Stonehenge, Wiltshire, is the Giant's Ring, it is easy to see how such stories might have gained currency. The giants, it seems, were displaced by a Trojan called Brutus; the land then was named after him, hence Britain.

Another story claims that Albia was the eldest of fifty daughters of a Syrian King. After killing all their husbands on their wedding night they were put aboard ship and left to the winds, which brought them to these

shores, where they settled down. A parallel tale has 33 daughters of Diocletian, the Roman emperor, doing the same.

Ptolemy mentions the name in Greek (Alouion, AD 127) as does Pliny later in Latin (Albion). Bede picks it up in the eighth century, simply saying '*Britain, formerly known as Albion*'. Michael Drayton, in his epic *Poly-Olbion* of 1613, claims Albion as a Christian martyr from Rome, the first in Britain. Now poetry keeps the name alive, together with pubs and proud football teams, such as Brighton and Hove Albion. West Bromwich

Albion (founded in 1879) notably was the first British team to welcome a high-profile triumverate of black players: Laurie Cunningham, Cyrille Regis and Brendan Baston – new giants for the 1980s.

The name Albion, as invoked by Peter Ackroyd, often devolves to England, seeming less territorial than poetical:

'Today, like those fading memorials, Albion is not so much a name as the echo of a name.'

ALEXANDERS

Migrants making their way inland, alexanders suddenly make an impact in April, when they fill coastal verges with their shiny, dark green leaves and umbelliferous yellow tops, looking healthy and happy at four feet tall.

You can't miss them around Lulworth, Dorset, where they ambush old boats. Near Watchet, Somerset they follow smugglers' footsteps towards Exmoor; in Norfolk they often refuse domestication inland but clamber exuberantly around the cliffs.

Probably introduced from the Mediterranean by the Romans as a vegetable, they were cultivated in monastery gardens and are still sometimes found nearby. A staple of cottage gardens, they go by the local names of angelica in East Anglia and wild celery on the Isle of Wight. Sometimes known as Parsley of Alexandria, they have become naturalised where they feel happiest, near to the southern coasts. Every part of the aromatic plant can be used, its roots being favoured by fishermen to augment soups.

AMMONITES

It would be strange if the presence of tiny snail-like and great bicycle-wheel coils of stone had not nourished stories in our inquisitive ancestors. Across the south of England, it was known that fairies who had been bad were turned into snakes and then into stone. 'Snakestones' in Whitby, Yorkshire and 'conger eels' on the Isle of Portland, Dorset were just some of the names given to fossils of extinct molluscs. The Egyptians, Greeks and Romans recognised rams' horns in these stones and, preoccupied as they were with sacred symbols, associated them with the god Amon.

Local tales give insights into a time before appreciation of the organic origin of petrified fauna and flora informed the discipline of geology. St Hilda took a novel approach when clearing the land to build a new convent in seventh-century Whitby, Yorkshire. The story goes that:

> *Of thousand snakes, each one*
> *Was changed into a coil of stone*
> *When holy Hilda pray'd*

SIR WALTER SCOTT, from *Marmion*

Indeed it is a great delight to wander the beaches of Yorkshire and come across a fist-sized nodule that can be broken open to reveal a perfect golden snake with its matching imprint. These creatures seemingly curling around their own tail do not possess a 'head'; this omission was rectified by local carvers, who added the necessary eyes and mouth for early tourists. *Hildoceras bifrons* – named for St Hilda – was a favourite for this. Today, three coiled shapes lie together in Whitby's coat of arms.

Whitby snakestone, Yorkshire.

St Keyna, who gives her name to Keynsham, Bristol (Radio Luxembourg fans will remember the spelling), is reputed to have petrified serpents long before St Hilda. What links the two is the geological formation of the Lias, from northern Yorkshire to Lincoln, Northampton, the Cotswolds, Somerset and down to Dorset.

The flat bedrock along the beach from Lyme Regis to Charmouth in Dorset entices with small and huge whorls smoothed by the relentless waves. It is also notable for fossil hunters. After every storm, since at least Georgian times, seekers of stones have followed attentively the sifting work of gravity and the sea. Here are found hundreds of different ammonites, sometimes glinting gold, vacuum-packed in iron pyrites. Mary Anning, the knowledgeable amateur palaeontologist and professional fossil seller, could distinguish two hundred in the early nineteenth century.

The scientific importance lies in finding ammonites in situ. Their rapid evolution, as they changed in size, shape, patterned striations and sutures, has been fundamental in giving us an idea of the sequence of events in the ebb and flow of the early Jurassic seas. Proto ammonites enter the stage in Carboniferous times (as goniatites), but it is in the Jurassic and Cretaceous that they reach their zenith and then extinction, together with the dinosaurs.

These free-swimming molluscs immigrated in numbers as the seas invaded. Their capacity to keep on changing made them the perfect time-tellers. The sheer profusion and variety of these coiled stones intrigued nascent geologists, who began to recognise that they could use specific species to correlate and date the sequence of sedimentary beds. They have helped to demonstrate nuances in the theory of evolution. The remarkable sequence of ammonites discovered in Southerham Grey Pit, near Lewes, Sussex, has recently enabled geologists to unravel the history of the early Lower Chalk as a greenhouse climate became established on earth, perhaps ninety million years ago.

Titanites giganteus from the Whit Bed on the Isle of Portland, Dorset reaches one metre in diameter; you can see them embedded into the walls of houses and gardens in Easton and Southwell. In Sussex they present a rustic counterpoint to the Regency reproductions of Lewes and Brighton. A builder called Amon Wilds so rejoiced in his given name that, on discovering the 'ammonite order' created by London architect George Dance – who decorated his Shakespeare Gallery on Pall Mall (1789) with ammonite motifs – he set about topping his own columns with elegant coils. The façade of 166 High Street in Lewes, and Brighton's Oriental Place, Hanover Crescent and Montpelier Crescent, still demonstrate his work and that of his son in the early nineteenth century.

ARCHES

Arches sculpted by weather and waves around our shores show great fortitude despite attack from every side. Perhaps this is what draws us to them; easily described, unambiguous points of reference, they are obvious landmarks for seafarers.

Bat's Head in Dorset has a fledgling arch, but the beautiful Durdle Door stands at the other end of the bay, west of Lulworth Cove. Linked to the mainland, this great gothic portal through Portland and Purbeck stone frames views of the sea. The isolated rocks of the Bull, Blind Cow, Cow and Calf are part of the same line of heaved limestone and foretell the fate of the arch.

Thurlestone Rock stands solitary in Bigbury Bay, Devon. Only when you walk to either end of the sands are you surprised and delighted by the realisation that this is a huge archway in the sea. The hard conglomerate mass is mentioned by name as a boundary marker in a Saxon charter dated 845, its resilience echoed in the local saying *'brave every shock like Thurlestone Rock'*. The rock is more than thirty feet high and the hole twenty feet; in 1864 it was said that *'the noise made by the wind rushing*

Durdle Door, Dorset.

through the archway is sometimes heard many miles away, and when it is perceptible at Kingsbridge it is regarded as the forerunner of storms of rain'.

The word thirl – occasionally used in north-country dialect for gate or hole – deriving from Old English *thyrhil* or Old High German *durhhil*, meaning pierced, is evident in both of these names. Etymological evidence alone suggests that these names are more than a thousand years old.

Older names exist. In Cornwall, Enys Dodman, an arch in obdurate granite, stands in the angry sea off Land's End; it has counterparts by Gribba Point and Carn Vellan. Enys, or ynys, means 'island' in Cornish, as in Welsh.

The kittiwakes make much of the challenge at Bempton Cliffs in Yorkshire, flying through the limestone arches like First World War aces. Blackhall Rocks include an arch visible at low tide along the Durham coast. Less resilient has proved the wonderfully stolid-looking limestone arch of Marsden Rock, County Durham. Several choirs gathered one hundred feet up on its top in 1903 to give an early rock concert; in 1911 there was a big rockfall, and over the years pieces have toppled; but in 1996 it lost its bridge to gravity. The totemic power of the arch was then further tamed as the smaller buttress was removed by blasting to make it 'safe', leaving just one square stack. This remodelling by nature and man has had an impact on local people – the silhouette they grew up with has been stolen.

Thurlestone Rock, Bigbury Bay, Devon.

At the western tip of the Isle of Wight, an arch split from the mainland in 1815, isolating another stack as part of the Needles. In Freshwater Bay, Arch Rock remains in name only; it fell in 1992. Back in Dorset, quarrying took the White Hole, a natural gateway near Portland Bill, in the 1870s, leaving a remnant known as Pulpit Rock.

Waves, searching every crevice often with explosive force, soon trace a weak line or bedding plane in a cliff face. In areas where geology has been much contorted, fracturing and cracking leave faults and joints often parallel and at right angles to one another; these are the perfect conditions for the formation of caves, possibly followed by arches.

Joining forces with the sea, aerial bombardment by rain, frost and wind ensures that arches are short-lived in geological time, the 'bridge' always vulnerable to gravity. The sequence runs from cave to arch to stack to heap to dispersal by the sea, but in between these rocks are endowed with personalities, stories and significance.

ARTISTS' COLONIES & SCHOOLS

The group we know as the Norwich School painted their beautiful medieval city and the extensive flatnesses of East Anglia at the start of the nineteenth century. John Sell Cotman sought national recognition, but John Crome remained around the banks of the river Yare, rooted in the landscape, once declaring to his pupils: '*This is our Academy.*' His invention of the Norwich Society of Artists in 1803, the first provincial group to be formed, was instrumental in galvanising a movement with learning and expression at its heart. This was born out of the city's own tradition of dissent and the welcoming of 'Strangers' seeking refuge from hostility across the North Sea. The gatherings were progressive, the painting innovative, despite conservative patronage and the turbulence of war – the focus on familiar landscapes offering reassurance while classical rules and subjects were routed. Their legacy is a rich vein of works by pupils, acolytes and masters, from Cotman's *Mousehold Heath* to Crome's *Moonrise on the Yare*, portraying fragments of Norwich, including its abbeys, mills, markets and river traffic.

London always attracted and harboured artists of all kinds. Different quarters have had their associations, such as Holland Park with its Royal Academicians. The alchemy of the aristocracy and upper middle classes – linking fashion and power – created an art market that Bond Street and the Academy still pursues.

Chelsea carried the banner for Bohemian living and expression (Rossetti, Whistler). Fitzroy Square waved no particular flag until the Slade School of Art two blocks east gained a progressive name at the turn of the twentieth century (Sickert, Gore, Augustus John). Camden emerged as the home of the avant-garde, until it progressed uphill to Hampstead with Sickert at its prow. In the decade before the Second World War, artists, architects and commentators, including Naum Gabo, Walter Gropius, Barbara Hepworth, Piet Mondrian, Henry Moore, Paul Nash, Ben Nicholson and Roland Penrose, although never forming a school, came together in Hampstead, nourishing local life and world art in an unprecedented way.

In the 1980s the East End was said to have ten thousand artists within a couple of miles of Old Street. Young architects and artists, like pioneering species, colonised down-at-heel, interesting corners in which to cheaply live and work. In the late 1960s Bridget Riley, Peter Sedgley and others inspired the creation of SPACE, an organisation to find and administer working places for artists. Their pioneering work began among the ghosts of vacated St Katharine Docks beside Tower Bridge. Newly graduating artists, desperate for space in which to create their bigger canvases and constructions, created ACME in 1972 to organise access to short-lease properties. Some campaigned unsuccessfully against the inevitable property developers, who began to see potential and profit spreading through the Wapping warehouses during the 1970s.

In 1975 the focus was moving towards Hackney, east London, particularly Beck Road, which became a haven for living and work as well as a crucible for the politics of housing. Many artists still live there. By the 1990s the scene had moved to Hoxton. Exhibitions and happenings invested these parts of the East End with New British Art glamour and brought people to places they never would have explored.

In parallel other artists left the city. The Ruralists, including Ann and Graham Arnold, Peter Blake, David Inshaw and Annie and Graham Ovenden, flourished as a group in Somerset in the 1970s. One hundred years earlier the Manchester School, following Joshua Anderson Hague, avoided the industrial engine of the city by taking frequent expeditions to north Wales, where they explored Impressionism.

The cosmopolitan nature of coastal settlements, however small, the light – a gift from the sea, cheap accommodation and the character of their huddled dwellings attracted those seeking a life free from social constraint. Staithes, a tiny fishing village in Yorkshire, drew towards the end of the 1800s the Northern Impres-sionists, excited by the naturalistic painting activities found in fashionable Brittany, France. Around the 1880s at Newlyn in Cornwall, Stanhope Forbes, Frank Bramley, Thomas Cooper Gotch, Norman Garstin and later Laura and Harold Knight settled, seeking the same experience of *en plein air* painting.

After *The Rain it Raineth Everyday* by Norman Garstin, 1889, Newlyn Old School.

To the north of the peninsula, St Ives had been home to artists since the 1870s. But it was with potters Bernard Leach and Shoji Hamada that a new phase began in the 1920s. By the start of the Second World War, Adrian Stokes, Ben Nicholson, Barbara Hepworth and Naum Gabo had moved here. Peter Lanyon was native born. Roger Hilton, Terry Frost and Patrick Heron arrived after the war. With the exquisite light particular to the Cornish coast, the sensuality of the land-forms, the Celtic heritage and standing stones, the local surroundings seeped into their work, together with the currents of modernist thought that were washing around the world.

Further enrichment was at work. No doubt given courage by the painting culture in the town, a Devonian seaman called Alfred Wallis began, at the age of 75, to paint ships and harbour using boat paint on scraps of board. His naïve eye and flattened perspectives palpably influenced Nicholson and others, though he died in poverty in the war.

St Ives artists survived through sales to tourists; now the town owes them a great economic debt as visitors come to see the places where they worked. With post-modernism has come the Tate Gallery St Ives, opened in 1993. Its very presence is part of the artists' legacy. It maintains the momentum begun in 1895 by Passmore Edwards's innovative benefaction of the Orion Art Gallery in Newlyn.

Positively remote from the metropolis, with nourishment brought for centuries by sea, Cornwall, with its palette of ancient rocks, wild weather, beguiling light, deep identity and tough lives, continues to feed the imagination.

BANDSTANDS

Bexhill's seafront has a bandstand, completed in 2002. It can be moved around on its small wheels in front of the marine lines of the De La Warr Pavilion, that unparalleled monument to modernism on the Sussex

The Quomps, Christchurch, Hampshire.

Mobile bandstand, Bexhill-on-Sea, Sussex.

coast. Against the backdrop of Mendelsohn and Chermayeff's lauded 1930s pleasure palace, the little mobile bandstand, by architect Niall McLaughlin and engineers Price and Myers, holds its own. It seems like a fragment of white sail, pinned down but billowing in the wind.

Most bandstands date from Victorian times. With public health and welfare, temperance and social control on their minds, city fathers opted for the creation of city parks and seaside pleasure grounds, in which the bandstand provided a vehicle for both passive diversion and active endeavour.

Many have an oriental feel. Elegant cast-iron posts and railings stand on circular or octagonal plinths, supporting slightly upturned low-pitched roofs with delicate lanterns and filigree ironwork. Some were particular to their place; in the South West some were thatched.

A singular bandstand was built in the newly laid-out Dartmouth Park in West Bromwich, Staffordshire, close to the iron foundries, in 1887. Some were designed by well-known architects: Francis Fowke, architect for the Albert Hall in London, designed bandstands for the Royal Horticultural Society in Kensington, London – one still functions after removal to Clapham Common. They soon became so popular that iron makers began to create standard patterns.

With reviving interest in the urban park, bandstands are being resurrected once more, such as the colourful and ornate bandstand in

Newcastle's Exhibition Park and the fine cast-iron bandstand on the Quomps in Christchurch, Hampshire.

BASKING SHARKS

From April to September, around the south-west peninsula, especially Cornwall, the world's second-largest fish can be seen feeding alone or in groups of a dozen or so. Growing as big as coaches, 35 feet long, basking sharks gently follow the plankton, swimming with their vast mouths open like windsocks, straining water through their special gills.

They congregate where the meeting of water fronts stirs up nutrients from the seabed and fuels a plankton bloom – off Lundy Island in the Bristol Channel, for instance. Occasional sightings are recorded on the north-east and north-west coasts, too. Recent research reveals that we have one of the world's largest populations off our shores, but it is moving northwards, following the plankton as the seas get warmer.

Despite protection up to twelve miles offshore, populations have declined by half in the past twenty years. Like so many other sea creatures, the basking shark is being seriously overfished – its six-foot dorsal fin is a delicacy in Chinese cuisine and its liver produces valuable oil.

BEACHES

Beaches attract us with the exhilaration of the freedom of 'the common'. But 55 per cent of the littoral zone is owned by estates, local authorities, statutory bodies, government departments and business interests that control large areas for energy production, oil refining and so on. The Crown owns the rest, although it leases some to ports and wildlife organisations.

One day a beach may have a simple, falling profile, for example along

Yorkshire's Holderness coast. The next it may have giant terraces redrawn by storm waves. Breakwaters erected to slow longshore drift make for exciting walking along the shore, with sand piled high up to one side and a big drop down to pools on the other, as at Clacton in Essex.

Chesil Beach in Dorset is a geological wonder of the world. A tombolo linking the mainland with the Isle of Portland, it stretches for eighteen miles, rising eastwards to forty feet in height. Along its length the pebbles are so predictably sifted that local fishermen can read their whereabouts in them: at Abbotsbury they are smaller than a Fisherman's Friend lozenge, while at Chiswell a single pebble is bigger than the hand. Thousands of little terns nest among the pebbles. It is dangerous for them, and illegal for walkers to wander here between 1 May and 31 August.

Winter walking is nowhere better than on the crunchy East Anglian stretches of shingle at Scolt Head, Blakeney Point and Orford Ness, with skeins of geese flying noisily above, or along the south coast, for example at The Crumbles, Sussex and Dungeness, Kent, with the groynes adding to the distractions at Selsey, Sussex. But there are scant amounts of shingle in the north.

Pure white sand may be of ground coral – calcium rich and useful in farming. But most sand is dominated by pure quartz; it will frost glass when blasted by the wind. Among the colours in a handful of sand the other constituent seen most easily is mica – shiny dark flakes, light in weight, that stick to the skin. Alum Bay on the Isle of Wight is famed for the many discrete sand colours created by erosion of the vertically tipped rocks.

Sara Hudston compares the sands in the Isles of Scilly, Cornwall. *'Scilly sand is white, palest palomino when wet, and full of sparkling mica. It varies in grade from*

Dawlish Warren, Devon.

island to island. St Agnes, the western-most inhabited place, has gritty sand that scrunches underfoot like coarse glass. Tresco's long flanks are heaped with fine powder. Bryher sand has the texture of table salt and St Martin's beaches are packed hard and clean. On St Mary's, sand from Porth Mellon was once considered so superior that parcels of it were sent as presents to the Mainland to blot the wet ink on letters and documents.'

Dramatic cliffs at Staithes and Robin Hood's Bay in Yorkshire are the backdrop for wave-cut platforms over flatbedded rocks revealed on the falling tide. In Somerset, at Kilve Pill, the oil shale strata are slightly tilted, offering a complex of tiers with necklaces of pools in which the locals once went 'glatting' for conger eels.

Small sandy coves offer a joyous combination of security and prospect. Polzeath Beach in north Cornwall has it all: soft, clean sand, splendid safe surf, cliffs, island, rock and sand pools, as well as simple facilities. The popularity of Bournemouth beach is due to sunshine and soft, clean sands, while Brighton draws the crowds because it is fashionable despite the pebbles.

Meanwhile, in the centre of London on a warm summer night, the river police may be heard shouting ashore that the tide is coming in and the Reclaim the Beach party begins to wind down. Between the Oxo Tower and the South Bank complex is a beach, contested for many years – this land is jealously championed by local people, despite the riverward push of shoreline development. Many have memories of relaxing on the beach created between 1934 and 1964 in front of the Tower of London. The rising tide of pollution and drownings eventually led to its being abandoned. But the great and positive story of the clean-up of the Thames may bring more made beaches, as in Berlin and Paris.

Sharing the beach with birds is a pleasure compounded by seasonal variations. The scurry of the rushing turnstone upending flotsam along the strand line, ridding us of sand-hoppers; the more considered actions of the oystercatcher probing for molluscs; a long-beaked curlew stretching a leg; these are not seen everywhere. The query 'Any stuff about?' as you pass someone with binoculars might bring you 'loads of avocets' on the Norfolk coast or in Northumberland 'the Arctic terns are back '.

BEACH HUTS

The prudish nature of Victorian bathing has left us a colourful legacy – the beach hut is a descendant of the wheeled bathing machines from which daringly clad men and women stepped down for a dip in the sea. Reminiscent also of simple bungalows, '*the verandah style probably owes much to the British Empire … India and the Caribbean*', says Tim Baber. There is also a great tradition in mainland Europe of the summerhouse or dacha.

Along parts of the coast, rag-tag gatherings of railway carriages, boats that have 'dunsailin', fishing huts and shacks link the land and the sea. Yorkshire, Cornwall, Essex and Devon all have their beach-hut fraternities. They bring twinges of jealousy to those who pass by the carefree domestic scenes featuring cups of tea and deckchairs, snoozing magazine readers and liberated tots with buckets and spades.

At Selsey, west Sussex, shingle-side plots originally squatted by makeshift buildings now support permanent brick and concrete. There are glimpses of old railway carriages; one has 'No Smoking' etched into its wood-framed windows.

Some beach huts cluster in wild corners, untamed, undesigned. But ranks of beach huts tend to be municipally owned and standardised, always in demand for hire by the season or the day. Where privately owned, rigidity of plot size and restrictive bylaws have not stifled the imagination. The variety and richness of decks and shutters, gable ends and roof lines, stilts and varnish make for seaside splendour even in winter.

Tim Baber's family owned a beach hut at Mudeford, Hampshire for more than fifty years. It was well equipped: '*A small solar panel fitted on the asphalt roof powered a laptop for the newspaper, a small television and a cassette player. Over the years almost any twelve-volt appliance invaded the place.*'

Wells-next-the-Sea, Norfolk.

It stands among a double line of 350 others, making a splash of colour and a zigzag of roofs along a sand spit that gives owners a dual outlook, inland over Christchurch Harbour and seaward towards the Needles. The sadness is that they have become real estate – Werere or Lazy Days may change hands for £140,000, even where the threat of rising sea levels is almost palpable and insecurity is only a storm away.

Local authority ownership should prevent the excesses of buying and selling, but controlled huts tend to regimentation and most allow no sleeping overnight. Some look like stable blocks for thin horses, as at Porthminster Beach in Cornwall, or like beach garages with padlocks, as at Hove, east Sussex. Further east at Bexhill-on-Sea, they range from pointed-roofed sheds to flat-roofed minimalist concrete, lively and colourful when occupied but unrelentingly white and introspective when not. Bournemouth owners have splashed theirs with primary colours. Along Shoebury beach in Essex every hut is different in size, shape and colour.

New lines of beach huts have been built during the past few years. The East Riding of Yorkshire retained Bauman Lyons Architects to refurbish Bridlington's South Foreshore Promenade. Working with the artist Bruce McLean they created a café, shops, boat slipways, paddling pool and viewing terrace linked by the mile-long promenade. Sculptures,

Bournemouth, Dorset.

water channels and a solar-heated shower add new dimensions to the seaside atmosphere, as do the robust, asymmetrically gabled beach huts, which have to be booked a year in advance.

At Whitstable, Kent, on the West Beach Promenade, double rows of former fishermen's huts have their own gardens. Some, two storeys high, are clearly lived in – old, black-painted lobster-pot and net sheds. Some of the huts at Southwold in Suffolk are like colonial bungalows for children. Others, still with gables to the sea and open balconies, are painted from a palette of deep blues, pinks and soft yellows normally seen only in sweet shops; some have carved fretwork gables and name boards – Dog Watch, Harry's Bar, Spunyarns. With ten steps leading up to a terrace, sometimes sideways on, the huts at Wells-next-the-Sea, Norfolk stand on stilts like welcoming bird boxes.

Kathryn Ferry has been studying beach huts. *'What particularly struck me as I travelled around the coast was the diversity of beach hut shapes and sizes within very small areas. For example, beside the flat expanse of Lincolnshire sands between Mablethorpe and Sandilands, the difference in ownership as well as the relative property prices on the land behind has caused a surprising variety of styles ... From flat-roofed concrete boxes and square, double-fronted chalets painted in blocks of glossy red, blue and green for hire at Mablethorpe, one can walk along the promenade past a line of Oriental-looking huts towards Sutton-on-Sea. These are among my favourite huts. Built of pre-cast concrete they have corrugated asbestos roofs in a sort of Chinese pagoda style. I appreciate that they don't sound too promising, but en masse they are superb. Further along on the Bohemia Promenade, this type gives way to private wooden huts with verandas and traditional seaside names, while towards the posher end of Sandilands, the emphasis is on a sea view, with the huts ranged gable to gable with large windows that glint in the sun.'*

BEACONS (COASTAL)

'One thousand poor fishermen in open boats, not daring to near the shore, with a hard gale from ENE and raining in sluices, till a large coal light was raised on Beadnell Point, when nearly one hundred boats run in and all got safe, to the inexpressible joy of their numerous poor families.'

John Wood recounted this incident in 1828 to Trinity House, and was thereafter permitted to show a light on Beadnell Point, or Ebb's Neuk, in Northumberland for the herring season from 25 July to Michaelmas. Church towers standing proud of flat land were also used for beacon fires or lanterns: at the fifteenth-century church of St Nicholas (patron saint of seafarers) in Blakeney, Norfolk an extra tower was built in the northeast corner for this purpose.

Coastal beacons come in many guises. Although help for seafarers night and day is now dominated by the Global Positioning System (GPS)

Jack in the Basket: Lymington Harbour, Hampshire.

Top marks: Lymington Harbour, Hampshire.

Selsey Bill, Sussex.

and radar, there is still a need for workaday 'road signs' to aid navigation into harbour. In Whitby, Yorkshire two cylinders, red and green for starboard and port, stand on wooden legs at the end of the jetties on either side of the harbour entrance. Day marks – big obelisks or triangles of stone, sometimes striped in red or black and white – mark in idiosyncratic form the entrance to creek or harbour. At Walton on the Naze in Essex stands a brick tower once nearly ninety feet high. At Heugh Hill on Holy Island, Northumberland the steel 'Black Beacon' shines a light at night and carries a red triangle as day mark; its partner Guile Point Light Beacon has a solar-powered light.

The simplest of fixed beacons are attached to buildings or driven into sand, mud or rock, and stand in the sea with a distinctive top mark attached to them. These silhouettes demarcate navigable channels or note hazards. Selsey Bill in Sussex is edged by poles topped with triangles enclosing vertical bars to note the ends of groynes lost under the high tide. In Hampshire, the Channel Pilot says: '*to approach the entrance to Lymington river in the deepest water, bring Jack-in-the-basket beacon in line with the Lymington church*'. The striped pole topped by an iron cage and a light sports its name, as do other beacons in the harbour – Tar Barrel Post, Cocked Hat, Bag of Halfpence – reinforcing the other-worldliness of the language of the littoral.

BLACKPOOL ROCK

Pink, minty rock with the name of a place running through it shouts seaside town, Blackpool in particular.

Made by boiling, cooling and pulling sugar, lettered rock may have been invented in the 1850s by a London confectioner and street vendor, who developed a technique for incorporating words into the sticks – his eclectic messages included 'Do you love me?', 'Lord Mayor's Day' and 'Sir Robert Peel'. But it was Ben Bullock, a miner and confectioner from Dewsbury, Yorkshire, who, while on holiday in Blackpool in

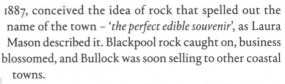

1887, conceived the idea of rock that spelled out the name of the town – '*the perfect edible souvenir*', as Laura Mason described it. Blackpool rock caught on, business blossomed, and Bullock was soon selling to other coastal towns.

In 1902 a sugar boiler who had worked for Bullock started his own rock factory in Blackpool. This marked the beginning of a thriving trade, with the opening of many factories and shops. In the 1930s, when the mills in nearby towns closed for the annual Wakes Weeks, Blackpool was full to the brim with holidaymakers and the factories worked to capacity, with itinerant sellers plying the beaches and streets.

During the Second World War, sugar rationing and loss of workers hit the factories. Women ran some of them: '*They did all the boiling, lettering and "rolling the lump", making smaller batches so they could handle the weight,*' Margaret Race wrote. Although prices rocketed, the rock remained as popular as ever. In the post-war years of sweet rationing, a thousand people patiently would form long queues to buy their holiday souvenirs.

According to Race, the 1950s were the '*boom time*', with up to fifty factories making the traditional sticks (mainly pink with red letters, but also multicoloured) as well as cat-faced lollipops and other rock novelties. Although the 1960s brought purchase tax on sweets, innovations, such as the move from wax paper to cellophane as a wrapping, enabled the factories to remain open and continue production all year round. In the late 1980s one to two thousand tons, made by seventeen producers, were sold every year in Blackpool alone.

Despite its cheapness, rock is largely handmade, and the sugar boilers are skilled operators – it takes five years to become '*completely competent*'. To make it, strips of red toffee are formed into letter shapes and wrapped around white sugar to form a very fat tube – about five feet long and up to twelve inches in diameter. This is rolled, spun and then stretched and stretched into thirty-foot strings, which are cut into bars.

Now rock is sold worldwide and has lost some of its cachet as the memory of a holiday. But if you go to the seaside you can't help buying some.

BLOW HOLES

Where weaker rock has given in to the harrying of the sea occasional roof collapses into wave-filled caves create constricted holes capable of exciting sound, water and air effects. The shape of the cave, the state of the tide and the depth of the swell compresses the air and the water to create and destroy these small wonders.

Game Victorian tourists were lured to hold out letters to be grabbed by air suction above the Devil's Letter Box in Kynance Cove, Cornwall, and wetly watch as great spouts of water were blown like whale breaths from the Devil's Bellows on Asparagus Island. The Blowing Hole of Porth Island puts on a display that can be seen from Newquay. The Lion's Den appeared near the Lizard Lighthouse in 1847 after the roof of a cave fell in.

With roar or gulp these 'gloops' fed the imagination of those who named them. Rumble Churn in Northumberland has been silenced by a rockfall, but the churn on Inner Farne Island can still steam up to a hundred feet in stormy weather. Near Flamborough Head in Yorkshire, Pigeon Hole contains the boiling sea.

BOATS

With such a varied coastline and rivers that make their way through diverse geology, it is inevitable that we should have perfected a wide range of inland and inshore boats for fishing and trading.

The first clue to the identification of a wooden boat lies in the method of joining the planks. Clinker-built boats rely on a small overlap of the timbers, a pattern that seems to have Viking origins and historically is found all the way from Berwick-upon-Tweed, Northumberland to Bournemouth, Hampshire. Originating in the Mediterranean, carvel-built boats rely on the abutting of timbers, giving a smooth finish to the hull; this way of building was practised from Purbeck, Dorset to the Solway Firth, Cumberland.

Eric McKee's wonderful *Working Boats of Britain* meticulously celebrates the diversity and aptness of our working wooden boats. He analysed the coastline by landscape, seascape, tidal range, fetch and degree of exposure to the wind and looked at the influence of surroundings, work and boatmen. In exploring the structures of boats, he observed that *'though one has to separate out the component elements, like climate, tide, fish, timber, and so on, for discussion, in reality they are interlocked in various mixtures peculiar to particular places'*.

One is drawn by the names, telling of their place of origin and work, such as Aldeburgh sprat boat, Hastings lugger, Norfolk wherry, Parrett flatner, Portland lerret, St Ives pilchard driver, Thames sailing barge and Whitstable oyster dredger.

All manner of nuances are noted by fishermen, boat builders and students, but even in the 1970s they agreed with McKee that variation, long honed, was diminishing: *'Boat building in wood is declining in favour of other materials such as metal, cement and petrochemicals, which have no local character.'* Later he conceded that *'as working boat designs move towards more general-purpose craft, their variety must decrease'*.

BORES

A bore (from the Old Scandinavian *bara*, meaning wave or billow) raises both exhilaration and fear in the heart as the full incoming force of a spring tide squeezed by narrowing riverbanks and a shallowing riverbed meets the outflowing water of a large river. They happen in several of our estuaries, the Solway in Cumberland, the rivers flowing into Morecambe

Bay in Lancashire, and the Trent in Nottinghamshire and Lincolnshire, where it is more likely referred to by the alternative name aegir.

The river Severn creates one of the most spectacular bores in the world. With a tidal range reaching fifty feet, second only to the 'Silver Dragon' of the Qiantang river in eastern China, the Bristol Channel in addition offers a narrowing funnel to the incoming tide. Close to the spring and autumn equinoxes, the spring tides are at their highest. Five-star bores are possible around the end of March and early in October, with lesser bores expected twice a day on four or five days every month, around the full moon. With a speed of ten miles per hour the wave front may reach six and a half feet; it achieved nearly ten feet at Stonebench, Gloucestershire on 15 October 1966.

Near Framilode, where the river is still quite wide, the 2003 spring bore was around three feet high – you could see it coming, quickly covering the exposed sandbars and propelling waiting canoeists upstream. Then came the noise – agitated lapping of waves against a sturdy defence wall. Suddenly the river was full of water, bringing up torn-out trees and other debris.

Most people congregate at Minsterworth, Stonebench and Over Bridge, where public access is easy. At bends in the river, the bore swooshes up and over the outside curves, sometimes engulfing cars on the road. Catherine Fisher captured a more benign mood, describing the river spilling its banks: '*slopping into the wellingtons of watchers, swamping the nests of coots, splashing binoculars*'.

This is a harsh environment for plants and animals, with two tidal changes every day and huge surges twice on sixty days of the year. The elver run was one of the wonders of the world, breathtaking in the sight and sheer quantity of tiny eels catching a ride and dealing with the ebb.

Although the numbers are nothing like they were, this is still the time when elver fishermen take their catch.

Others use the natural energy to their advantage. F. W. Rowbotham recorded that '*Severnside men of Minsterworth, Elmore Back and lower down in my earlier years would take their boats, ride out the bore and let the flood stream carry them to Gloucester; they would do their shopping and drift home on the ebb*'.

The sport of bore surfing is made the more thrilling and dangerous by the unpredictability of the surge. It has a longer history than one may expect, as Rowbotham recalled: '*at 10.30am on 21st July 1955, Colonel Churchill swam from the bank below Stonebench with his surfboard ... as the fair sized bore approached, the Colonel placed his board beneath him and began to swim upstream. Moments later the leading slope of the bore slid under him and he started planing forward.*' The members of the Severn Bore Riders Club are inspired by such pioneers. Dave Lawson holds the world distance surfing record: on 29 August 1996 he rode the bore for forty minutes, covering 5.7 miles.

THE CHANNEL

Claimed on these shores as the English Channel, but La Manche to the French, the Channel is an ancient riverbed that has evolved into an ever-changing sea. Linking the North Sea and the Atlantic Ocean, this unpredictable waterway has been central to our evolution. Both barrier and vital corridor, the Channel is replete with contradictions. When travel by water was easier than by land (or air), it united more than it divided, yet remained a source of patriotic pride as a barrier.

Invasion, or the threat of it, has long been central to the Channel's symbolic life. Pompey dismissed the Channel as an insignificant mud-flat, Napoleon considered it a '*ditch to be jumped*'. To Shakespeare, however, in the wake of the defeat of the Spanish Armada, it was '*a moat defensive to a house*'. Small yachts and oil tankers treat it with respect. Today it is prob-

ably the busiest shipping channel in the world, with ferries running like buses between French and English ports and crossing through traffic from the Baltic and Atlantic. Underneath lies a multitude of telecommunications cables, the oldest dating from the Victorian era, and a rail tunnel – the world's longest undersea construction, completed in 1993 after a century of debate and trial borings.

'England's white cliffs are more conspicuous from France than is the French shore from Britain,' wrote Michael Bonavia, a railway man who directed an abortive attempt to build a tunnel under the Channel in the 1970s. *'In fine weather, Dover's residents, however, can enjoy reading the time of day through a telescope focussed on the town hall clock in Calais.'*

Covering some thirty thousand square miles and a hundred miles at its widest at Finisterre, the Channel is at its narrowest just 21 miles from France, at the Strait of Dover, stretching from Dungeness to South Foreland in Kent. In the Strait, the water is shallow, 220 feet at most. Yet unique tidal streams, strong winds and heavy sea fogs that arise with disconcerting suddenness can make navigating the Channel a challenge. Between November and February, winds of force seven or eight can be expected on up to fifteen days a month, accentuating the short, steep waves so dreaded by travellers. Humps in the seabed add to the hazards – the Varne bank, midway between Cap Gris Nez and Dover, for instance, lies thirty feet below the surface at high tide and is marked by a lightship.

The Channel was cut by a massive European river system, the Greater Seine, as it flowed west into the Atlantic. But at various times during the past few thousand years, as the climate in the middle Pleistocene fluctuated between warm and cold spells, a ridge of chalk joined England to the continental landmass, enabling migrants – human and non-human – to recolonise the land when ice retreated. The first humans are believed to have walked here some half a million years ago, dated from fossil fauna and flint hand-axes recently discovered at Boxgrove in west Sussex.

The last important cold period was at its height thirteen thousand years ago, when a sheet of ice three-quarters of a mile thick sat over Scotland and north-west England. As the climate warmed over a few thousand years, hunter-gatherers crossed the North Sea and the Channel, still dry because of low sea levels. But as more ice melted, the landmass began to recover from the weight, rising in Scotland and the South East but tilting into the sea in the South West. Britain became an island again around eight thousand years ago.

The Channel west of the Solent remains distinctly different from its eastern reaches in Kent and Sussex, where medieval harbours, at Rye and Winchelsea, for instance, were stranded by a retreating coastline. Ports in the west, meanwhile, such as Southampton, Portsmouth, Dartmouth and Plymouth, prospered, especially as trade with the Americas developed.

Long the domain of fishermen, the Channel is now being dredged for sand and gravel to meet rising demand for concrete to build roads and houses in the South East. Plans are under way to mine some two hundred million tons from the Median Deep, midway between the Sussex coast and northern France. Such substantial damage to the sea-bed will harm fisheries, other marine life and archaeology, which is entering a new phase. English Heritage has begun an exciting three-dimensional survey of territorial waters in the Channel and North Sea, which might show ancient settlements and throw light on artefacts that are occasionally brought up in nets.

CHINES

In past times landing contraband and smuggling it inland must have been easier under the cover of the steep, woody ravines through soft, sandy cliffs that are peculiar to the Dorset, Hampshire and Isle of Wight coasts. Chines were eroded by short, small streams after the Ice Age and made more precarious by clay slides. In Poole and Bournemouth they are more domesticated, filled since Victorian times with rhododendrons and pines. John Betjeman captured their spirit: '*Walk the asphalt paths of Branksome Chine/ In resin scented air like strong Greek wine.*'

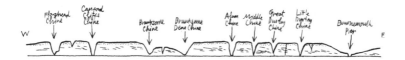

There are nineteen chines on the southern side of the Isle of Wight; a dozen between Shanklin and Freshwater, with names such as Shippards, Cowlease, Ladder, Blackgang and Shanklin, which has a dramatic forty-foot waterfall. From the air some look like little rifts, others are great clefts, yawning gaps, exactly what the word *cinan* meant in Saxon. On the ground they are exciting, small-scale landscapes, some grazed, some wooded, rumpled with landslips, always changing, perfect for exploring. At Mackerel Rail people stood lookout on the cliff top for fish, shouts going down to the beach for the boat to encircle the shoal with a seine net, which could be pulled in to the shore. In 1758 a 63-foot whale was marooned here and the name changed to Whale Chine. The chine itself is changing; recent landslips have cut off steps to the beach.

These southerly secret valleys are often the first landfall for migrating birds in spring, affording them shelter and food before they travel on. Butterflies also find them, and sea pink, bird's-foot trefoil and rock sea spurrey tempt other visitors, too.

CHOUGHS

In England the chough lives more in our imagination, folklore and heraldry than in reality. If you are fortunate enough to see one of these striking black, red-legged, red-billed members of the crow family, you are likely to be on the cliffs of Cornwall. As a result of persecution they had deserted the coasts of Sussex, Kent, Hampshire, the Isle of Wight, Somerset, Northumberland and north-west England by the end of the nineteenth century.

Even in Cornwall their numbers are few. They have been strongly associated with the county and with Arthurian legends – it is said that the soul of King Arthur migrated into a chough. There are many Cornish names for the bird – Cornish chough, Cornish daw, Cornish jack, Cornish jay, Cornish kae, killigrew and Market Jew crow (after the old name for Marazion, where they congregated). It appears on the county's coat of arms and in the Duchy of Cornwall's emblem.

The chough, pronounced 'chuff', stopped breeding in Cornish cliff-top caves and deserted buildings in 1952, but individual birds were seen performing their amazing aerial manoeuvres, riding the updraughts, until 1974. Then they left, as the cliff-top ecology changed, mainly due to changes in agriculture.

The birds need a short grass sward so that their long, curved bills can probe for insect larvae. Ten years of improving the habitat for the chough along parts of Cornwall's coastline, by reintroducing cattle-grazing right up to the cliff edge, has encouraged the bird to return to breed on the Lizard peninsula. First sighted in summer 2001, a breeding pair hatched three broods of four chicks in three years, watched around the clock to keep egg collectors at bay.

Since 1380 the chough has also featured on the City of Canterbury's coat of arms and three choughs appear on Thomas à Becket's arms. It was a Royalist symbol during the Civil War, which may explain The Three Choughs as a pub name, for example in Blandford Forum, Dorset.

CLIFFS

'The cliff coasts of Great Britain should be reckoned one of the country's most treasured possessions, they are of every variety and form, including the great chalk promontories of Flamborough Head and Beachy Head, the granite masses of Land's End, the sandstones of St Bee's Head … the newer limestones, sandstones and clays of Dorset, and the glacial cliffs of Holderness and Norfolk,' J. A. Steers wrote.

Cliffs offer the closest thing we have to wilderness in England, for here nature is in charge and there is little we can do to halt the inexorable processes of sea and tempest. About a fifth of England's coastline – some 750 miles – consists of cliff. Here an extraordinary array of the earth's ancient history is exposed to view: layered, tilted, folded, faulted rock forms of many kinds stand not only in vertical faces but as natural sculptures, from pillars, stacks and buttresses to arches and caves.

Most of our cliffs range from 150 to 300 feet in height. Boulby Cliff on the Yorkshire coast is our highest length of coastline, layers of Liassic shales and sandstones and boulder clay rising to 650 feet. Hard-rock cliffs that are nearly vertical, and hence tricky for humans, provide relatively safe breeding places for seabirds, although in the past people found ways to harvest these colonies. In the nineteenth century climbers, or 'climmers', took thousands of seabird eggs from nests along the Yorkshire coast at Bempton Cliffs.

Flamborough Head and Bempton Cliffs support England's only, and Britain's biggest, mainland gannet colony, as well as one of the largest kittiwake colonies in the North Atlantic. The sandstone cliffs of St Bees Head on the Cumbrian coast host England's only breeding colonies of black guillemots, as well as fulmars, kittiwakes, razorbills, cormorants, puffins and shags.

Plants also enjoy the freedom cliffs offer from grazing and competition. Ledges and crevices provide opportunities for hardy plants, such as rock sea-spurry and rock samphire, as well as lichens. But they have had to learn to live with wind and sea spray. The magnesian limestone cliffs at Hart Warren in County Durham support eight species of orchid, as well as moonwort, grass-of-Parnassus and bird's-eye primrose. The Lizard in Cornwall has an international reputation for its distinctive flora growing on serpentine rock.

The botanical diversity of all these cliffs is put to good use by butterflies, such as the chalkhill blue, holly blue, Lulworth skipper along the Dorset coast, and Glanville fritillary, confined to the disturbed cliff-face vegetation of the Isle of Wight. Short-tailed voles thrive on ungrazed cliff slopes and bats colonise caves and clefts along the mixed cliffs of Dorset: greater horseshoe, Beckstein's, Daubenteon's, Naterer's, whiskered and the very rare mouse-eared bat are all found there. On broken cliffs, adders, common lizards and slow-worms make a home, while the now rare sand lizard persists on soft, sandy, south-facing cliffs around Bournemouth.

Modern geology was forged in part by men and women who scoured the crumbling cliffs of Dorset, spurred by finds of long-extinct life forms in the rocks later defined as Jurassic, with exposures growing steadily older towards the west. Local fossil hunters still find prime specimens of ancient marine reptiles below these cliffs; they are on sale at fossil shops in Lyme Regis and Charmouth.

Many places offer particular views of the earth's crust, highly prized by geologists. Thanks to its cliff face, Kimmeridge Bay in Dorset gives its name to a particular period of geological time: rocks deposited anywhere in the world between 145 and 154 million years ago are said to be of Kimmeridgian age. Dinosaurs, such as iguanodon, turn up on the soft cliffs of the Isle of Wight, drawing a modest tourist trade. From the London clay in Essex and Kent, fossil shark's teeth spill out onto the beach.

Sea cliffs have been quarried in the past – near Whitby in Yorkshire for alum; Portland in Dorset for its prized building stone. In north Cornwall at Barrett's Zawn, slate was drawn through a now-collapsed tunnel to be loaded onto boats.

Between Flamborough Head and the Thames estuary stretches our flattest coastline, but there are cliffs of banded red chalk at Hunstanton, Norfolk and low cliffs of Pleistocene sand, gravels and boulder clay near Cromer and along the Holderness coast in Yorkshire.

Soft cliffs formed of shale or boulder clay slump as they erode, and the mosaic of habitats is readily colonised by plants. Only 160 miles remain free from coastal defences. Once stabilised, naturally or artificially, the natural mosaic of habitats is destroyed, as scrub takes over and nearby beaches, starved of sediment, start to disappear. During the past century, sea defences have probably reduced the flow of sediment from cliffs to coastal beaches by as much as fifty per cent. Current conservation wisdom is erring on the side of nature: increasingly cliffs are being left to retreat.

COASTGUARD COTTAGES

The view is stupendous, out over the sea and the coast for miles and miles. The circumstance is isolated, but a single wall embracing a terrace of houses with tall chimneys and their gardens make a little world

somehow safe from the raiding wind. With their towers or lighthouses, these were literal lookout points, places where the sea was scanned night and day for invasion fleets, boats in peril and smugglers who had made it past the customs boats.

The Preventative Water Guard was formed in 1809, superseded by the Coast Guard in 1822. Coastguards were posted away from their home towns to prevent collusion with smugglers, so the coastguard stations had to be built with living quarters to accommodate single and married officers. By 1839 more than four and a half thousand coastguards were in service.

An iconic image of Sussex, reproduced on countless postcards and tourist brochures, shows the sea, the white cliffs of the Seven Sisters and a row of gleaming white coastguard cottages in the foreground. These dwellings, perilously perched on the cliff above Cuckmere Haven, may now be private retreats for wealthy urbanites, yet they domesticate the wild landscape. Up the coast at Birling Gap, another lonely outpost with magnificent views across the Channel is fighting for its existence. Built in 1878, the eight cottages are being allowed to crumble into the voracious sea; at least two have been demolished for safety's sake. The National Trust, which has taken on many coastguard cottages, is following a policy of allowing natural realignment, despite local opposition.

Dunwich Heath, Suffolk.

COASTLINE

What is this coast? Horizon. Strand
With no beginning and no end,
A line, rewritten hour by hour,
The tale we tell about ourselves.

KATRINA PORTEOUS, from *Turning the Tide*

The shape of Britain is defined by the sea, but England has never been an island. Few of us can picture other than Britain, with the high head of Scotland, bulging gut of East Anglia, dragging cloak of Cornwall and Wales. Isolated, England seems unfinished where it marches with Wales and Scotland. The shift in shape is hard to come to terms with; part edged by sea, part bound by land.

While the political redrawing of boundaries goes on, the real work of flux is practised by the sea, making and breaking the rocks, plotting and piecing the edges, creating the richest of natural moats, chivvying and harrying anything 'man made'.

The geological past has seen massive alterations. Ancient tectonic territory crunching, along a line from Berwick-upon-Tweed to the Solway Firth, affirms that we are floating in a sea of deep and solid rock slowed by the grating together of bits of the landmasses of Gondwana and Laurentia some four hundred million years ago. A few hundred thousand years ago the ebbing and flowing of ice chased people away, and only eight thousand years ago we were northern Europe's bulwark to the Atlantic, being joined by land across what became the North Sea and the Channel. People, beasts and plants moved across this land bridge as the tundra and ice withdrew to the north. But from that defining moment, when the sea broke through, only things that could swim or fly, float on sea or wind or make boats could make it to our shores. Some things stopped coming until we carried them.

Jonathan Raban quoted Hilaire Belloc: '*Nowhere does England take on personality so strongly as from the sea.*' Raban wrote of '*the high excitement of making a landfall as the coastline across the water slowly thickens and takes shape … The land surfaces lazily out of the sea, first grey and indistinct, then flecked with hazy colour, then decorated with a sudden scatter of sharpening details – a broad scoop of chalky cliff, a striped beacon like a stick of candy, a continuous waterfall of slate roofs down the slope of a valley.*'

This is a small land both made vulnerable and protected by the sea. Most of us would have shared John Clare's childhood notion of space, imagining 'that the world's end was at the 'orizon and that a day's journey was able to find it'. Our view of the world would hardly have been shaped by maps until the nineteenth century, with the coming of the Ordnance Survey and universal education. Two hundred years later the assertion of our neighbouring countries and the contraction of the state requires a perceptive reworking of who we are and where we live. How long will it take to know our new skin – the outline of England?

COASTS

England's diverse and dynamic coastline stretches some five thousand miles. Taken twelve miles out to sea – the limits of British sovereignty – it covers seventy thousand square miles, nearly the size of England's total land area.

Every foreshore is unique. '*There is an atmosphere which only the sea can produce, a nautical tang, a seaside flavour,*' Kenneth Lindley wrote in 1967. '*Every mile of coast, every square foot of beach has its own character. Most of it exerts its own peculiar attraction. Nothing like it can be found inland.*'

Sand, carried by currents and blown by the wind, varies from beach to beach. Walk a few feet along a natural shingle coast and the nature of the pebbles changes. Forensic study shows that the precise mix of tiny rock grains and minute shell fragments found in one place is never repeated in another.

Shingle makes up about a third of the coastline, with many shingle banks occurring in the South and South East, the largest at Dungeness in Kent. Vegetated shingle banks are scarce in Europe and this is one of six large examples in England. At Foulness in Essex are the largest shell banks in the country; these so-called sub-fossil accumulations form part of one of the largest inter-tidal flats in Britain. Seven species of birds visit in internationally important numbers and there are breeding colonies of little, common and sandwich terns.

Our many offshore islands and sandbanks, big and small, provide refuges for birds and sea mammals. The Farne Islands in Northumberland are famous for their grey seals and nesting bird colonies. Hilbre, Roa, Foulney, Walney and Piel Islands, the Isle of Wight, Lundy, Steepholme, Flatholme, Bryher, Samson, Tresco, St Martin's, St Mary's, St Agnes, Holy Island, Coquet Island, St Mary's Island, Read's Island, Brownsea Island, Burgh Island, St Michael's Mount and many more add length and richness to our coastline.

Our estuaries are *'unrivalled anywhere in Europe for their diversity and, in wild life terms, are quite outstanding,'* Andrew Cooper wrote. Vital for industry and shipping, sixteen million people live around them. After Sydney, Australia, Poole Harbour is the world's second-largest natural harbour. The river Severn has the second-highest tidal range. Rias, a particular and beautiful feature of the south-west coasts, are drowned river valleys. Morecambe Bay, the Wash and the Thames estuary have three of our most extensive salt marshes, important places for wading birds, where vast expanses of sand are uncovered at low tide. Coastal lagoons sound exotic, but we have more than a hundred around the English coast, notably the Fleet behind Chesil Bank in Dorset.

There are fine sand-dune systems at Braunton Burrows in Devon, Ainsdale in Lancashire and on Lindisfarne and at Ross Links,

Northumberland. At Studland on the Isle of Purbeck you may come across naturists, whereas at Ainsdale, in the slacks, you may find (at night) a running toad with a yellow stripe down its back. Known as the natterjack, it is called locally Southport nightingale and Bootle organ, owing to its nocturnal chorusing.

The rocky shores of Cornwall, built of solid granite, resist the force of the sea, but crevices and pools abound on soft shores of slate or shale. The easily eroded mudstone cliffs of Dorset still reveal fossil ichthyosaurs and plesiosaurs, reptiles that swam in the Jurassic sea. As soft cliffs disintegrate they release stones and finer sediment, which travel along the coast during the relentless process known as longshore drift, providing raw material to build salt marshes, sandy beaches, dunes and shingle.

Chalk shores, at Flamborough in Yorkshire, Hunstanton in Norfolk and, most spectacularly, along much of the coasts of Kent, Sussex, Dorset and the Isle of Wight, are rare in Europe; England lays claim to nearly two-thirds of the continent's coastal chalk. Soft, and liable to crumble away from the cliffs, chalk supports a distinctive array of plants and animals, including molluscs, sponges that can bore into the rock, and green seaweeds found on no other type of rock.

All along the coast, attempts to control these natural forces have led to unforeseen and unwanted consequences, ultimately starving beaches of replenishing sand, sediment or pebbles, or leaving them more vulnerable to erosion. The remnants of the fishing village of Hallsands in south Devon stand as a monument to the folly of interfering with the sea. Once, the village was protected by a large pebble ridge, but it was destroyed by a January storm in 1917 after more than half a million tons of sand and gravel had been dredged offshore to extend the naval dockyards at Plymouth.

It is now known that extracting sand and gravel from beaches results in more wave energy reaching sea cliffs or sea defences, undermining them. Inappropriate coastal defences and the dredging of shipping channels have starved estuaries of sediment. Solid coastal defences can

deflect wave energy back, eroding sediment and causing a beach to disappear. Removing sea walls to allow salt marsh and mud-flats to adopt their natural form will start to compensate for some of the losses.

Divers in the cold English sea visit a world as important and colourful as any tropical reef, populated by corals, kelp forests and a seabed teeming with some forty thousand species. Rocky landscapes hide under the sea as well, particularly around the Farne Islands in the North East. Diversity in England's underwater life is heightened by the presence of colder northern waters that give way to warmer southern ones. Transition zones lie at Flamborough Head in the North Sea and along the English Channel, although this is changing with global warming. Species with demanding requirements choose their place along the continuum.

For instance, a beautiful coral called the pink sea fan, more typically a denizen of Mediterranean waters, is found only off the coast of south-west England, while the cold-water-loving bottlebrush hydroid sticks to the east coast, venturing no further south than Flamborough Head. The health of these species, together with that of the cold-water herring in the North Sea and the pilchard off Cornwall, is being monitored as climate change affects sea temperatures. We are learning about the richness around us just as it is diminishing through our own actions.

Lundy Island in Devon is England's first official 'no-take zone', with support from local fishermen. A little more than a square mile has been set aside to create a refuge for fish, shellfish and corals, such as the pink sea fan. But elsewhere, fishermen using beam trawls and scallop dredges

Selsey, Sussex.

damage large areas of the seabed. Even rocky coasts can now be harvested with so-called rock-hopper trawls. Further disturbance comes from large-scale marine sand and gravel extraction, mostly off East Anglia, Kent and Sussex – each year 23 million tons are removed from the seabed.

In the open sea off England's coasts, basking sharks follow the plankton bloom. Leatherback turtles swim in warmer English waters in search of their jellyfish prey, but often fatally take plastic bags by mistake, or drown after becoming tangled in lobster- and crab-pot lines. Dolphins hunt in the English Channel, where a large number of their deaths have been linked to pelagic trawling for bass. In the North Sea, harbour porpoises are killed by mid-water trawls. The mammals are dying at a rate estimated to result in their decline and eventual loss from our waters. Worse, scientists believe that the North Sea's ecosystem is on the brink of collapse.

Thirty per cent of us live within six miles of the coast, and every year half the population visits at least once. When a Lewes doctor, Richard Russell, published his '*dissertation concerning the use of sea water in diseases of the glands*' in 1750, he helped to spark the development of Brighton as a bathing resort, attracting the patronage of the aristocracy. Beachcombing and sea bathing developed as respectable middle-class pursuits in the Victorian era, combining healthful exercise with morally improving nature studies. Piers and well-lit promenades along the sea, at Southend-on-Sea in Essex and Blackpool in Lancashire, attracted thousands by day and night. By the 1880s the Great Eastern Railway Company was offering Londoners cheap weekend returns to Cromer and Yarmouth on the Norfolk coast.

Our love affair with the sea extends cautiously to its bounty: kippers from Craster, Northumberland; cod landed at Grimsby, Lincolnshire; mackerel from Brixham, Devon. But the dramatic loss of fish from our waters is changing the lives of people and settlements that have lived and died by the sea.

COBLES

Under a big, rectangular, dipping lug sail the coble sends a Viking reverberation down the spine. Indeed, in north Northumberland it is popularly understood that the Norse longship informs the design of this inshore fishing boat.

From Humber to Tweed graceful cobles work directly from the beach, where a gaggle of salt-rusted tractors lie waiting to haul them up the sand. The boat is narrow fore and aft, but is shallow and wide-bellied to withstand the rigours of landing on the sand. It is clinker-built for lightness, with strength to launch into crashing waves and stand up to the intense squalls and storms of the North Sea.

Bill Smailes from Craster described the nuances of making this boat to Katrina Porteous: '… if you go and order a coble, you give them the length of the ram plank and they build it from that. The ram plank is the bottom centre one that runs from just forrard of the engine, aft to the centre bottom of the stern. That plank is generally 22 to 24 feet in length. If it is 26 feet you will get a big, clumsy coble, impossible to work with on a beach.' He goes on to describe the long timbers of larch that are copper-nailed and riveted, then the inside frame: 'oak or elm is used up the side, and they are cut from crooked pieces of tree grown roughly to that shape naturally. They are much stronger than if they had been artificially shaped. These pieces take a lot of fitting, and it takes a craftsman to do it. I hope it won't all be lost.'

All the coastal villages had a fleet, often painted in a middle shade of blue, with fine Roman lettering. A few fishermen still work out of Beadnell in these traditional boats, now fitted with engines. In Yorkshire, where the pronunciation has shifted from 'ceoble' to 'cobble', the coastal conditions have varied sufficiently for small shifts in design. Some are double ended for launching into waves, as at Redcar, where they were differentiated as 'cockton'.

Although a few are being built, all by eye rather than formally designed, each year the numbers of these beautiful boats dwindles. The Filey coble, for example, fell in numbers from 190 to seventeen in the hundred years to 1984; by 2000 there were just five. As a demand of decommissioning, simply to prove to the government that the boat is no longer being used for fishing, they are burnt on the beach.

CORNISH GIGS

As a vessel returning from the Americas or Australia entered Cornish waters she would be met by gigs racing out from the Isles of Scilly or the mainland. The winning gig would get the work of piloting the vessel through the treacherous seas. Built for speed and manoeuvrability, pilot gigs are light, narrow, clinker-built boats, around 32 feet long and four feet, nine inches or more across the beam. Powered by six oars, they risk the sea in all weathers and can reach speeds of nine knots. Stories are told of further use as lifeboats and for long-distance visits to France for contraband.

This tradition of hard competition is now matched in the thriving sport of pilot-gig racing. Originating in Cornwall and the Isles of Scilly, it has increased in popularity since the 1980s and is beginning to spread along the south coast and across the world. More than forty clubs gather for competition from March to October, with exciting and colourful races for men, women, youths and veterans. The World Championship gig races draw teams from as far away as Australia, America, The Faroes, France and Holland.

The oldest boats date from the early nineteenth century. The Newquay, for example, built in 1812, is still raced from its home harbour, and the Treffry, dating from 1838, is used as the design blueprint for speed and fitness in these waters. A revival of boat building has been sparked, with small-leaved Cornish elm, *Ulmus stricta*, being used for planking and silver spruce replacing ash for the eighteen-foot oars.

COUNTIES

In 1974 Avon, Cleveland, Cumbria, Merseyside, Humberside, South Yorkshire and the West Midlands stared back at us from administrative maps. Greater London had appeared in 1965. Rutland, Huntingdonshire, Westmorland, East Yorkshire and Middlesex – *'that most hardly used of all counties'*, as Betjeman put it – seemed to evaporate, and other parts of the familiar jigsaw changed shape. But many of us had not moved an inch and the unsettling truth became clear two decades later, when things changed again – these were just passing clouds. Our 'real' counties, 39 shapes, historic bounds of cultural life and identity, had never gone away.

The Association of British Counties has persuaded us of the usefulness of discerning between counties (historic counties), administrative counties and ceremonial counties (the domain of the Lord Lieutenant, which in Derbyshire, for example, includes the City of Derby). All are constructs, but the historic counties tell us about deep identity, having earned credibility through continued use over a thousand years or more. Kent is the oldest entity to be recorded, first in 55BC, the land of the Cantii tribe, whose name could come from Celtic *canto*, an edge or rim (geographically appropriate), or from *caint* – 'open country'.

As Oxford and Cambridge blues compete along the Thames, reference to the Middlesex side and the Surrey side reminds us of the historic configuration, the boundary between the people of the Middle Saxons and the people of Suthrige – the region south of the Thames. Rivers and hills are often taken as borders and boundaries. But there are traces of old political rivalries, too, some of which may reach back to Celtic times.

As Norman Davies writes: '*The transformation of the chaotic patchwork of statelets into a map containing fewer but much larger and more integrated political cultural units was the work of half a millennium. It was not a foregone conclusion. Through a thousand military conflicts, marriages, mergers and mishaps, the teeming territories of the fifth century amalgamated in the course of two hundred years to form a dozen rival kingdoms. After two hundred years more, the kingdoms of the seventh century had been still further reduced, leaving two distinct zones – one predominantly Celtic, the other exclusively Germanic.*'

In the Germanic zone, smaller units – Saxon *scirs* (shires) and Norse *jarldoms* (earldoms) under the Danelaw – appear in written documents: for example, East Seaxe (Essex) in 604; Beaurrucsir (Berkshire), referring to a wooded hill, in 860; Scrobbesbyrigscir (Shropshire) – the shire of Shrewsbury, Latin Civitas Scrobbensis, 'the city around the scrub folk' – in 1006.

The counties of England emerged out of the Norman administrative system, based in most of the country on these shires or provinces, arranged around kings, upon peoples and obligations of providing soldiers and taxes. The lands of the middle, south and east Saxons were governed as the shires of Middlesex, Sussex and Essex; the 'folk of the north and south' were resolved into the shires of Norfolk and Suffolk. Wessex under Alfred had long been divided into smaller *scirs*. The Celts were confined by the Saxons to the 'land of the foreigners' – Kerno, kern-wealh or Cornwall. Northumbria and Yorkshire were already defined and the Mercian midlands had been divided in the tenth century. As he drew the country together, all William the Conqueror had left to delineate were Durham, Cumberland, Westmorland, Lancashire and Rutland, with his counts at their helm.

And so the county remained for centuries, persisting for the most part through the Victorian invention of a new administrative system with elected members, but with cities now jostling for power. Closer to our time, years of debate over what to put where was resolved by a change of government in 1970. The Conservatives recoiled from radical rewriting

The historic counties.

of administrative boundaries and settled for a partial and inconsistent rejigging. In 1974, when new two-tier structures and unitary authorities appeared, people felt their counties had been dismembered.

Lancastrians were upset by the inclusion of Lancashire, North of the Sands, in Cumbria. Confusion persists. In criticising Common Ground's england-in-particular.info website, gazetteer Michael Dutson was more restrained than some: *'Lancastrians are proud of their county and its achievements and we do get a little miffed with people who fail to recognise the seven-hundred-plus-year-old county of Lancashire in preference to a county that existed for only fourteen years.'*

Steve Sherdley kept up the pressure and told us about Lancashire Day. *'People have assumed that Lancashire places have "moved", so that Southport is now thought of as Merseyside, Hawkshead is thought of as Cumbrian, Wigan Greater Manchester and Warrington Cheshire, etc.'* The celebrations on 27 November remember 1295, when the first elected representatives of the county entered King Edward I's Model Parliament. Chris Dowson adds that red roses are worn and proclamations are read by town criers *'from the Furness Fells to the River Mersey, from the Irish Sea coast to the Pennines'*.

It is likely that administrative counties will be changed again as regions begin to assert their power and attempt to market themselves. It will fall to those who keep writing Middlesex on their letters, strong followings of friends, such as for Huntingdonshire, Lancashire and the smallest county for which we all have an underdog kind of fondness – Rutland – to demonstrate ways of maintaining their presence in the twenty-first century.

COVES

A small wonder of the world, Lulworth in Dorset is the dream cove. It takes you straight to adventures with George, Anne, Julian, Dick and Timmy, solving mysteries involving *'Brandy for the Parson,' 'Baccy for the*

Clerk'. The land almost completely embraces the water; from the land the glimpse of the open sea is overwhelmed by the intimacy and security of the bay.

This is the geomorphological archetype: hard rock broken through, enabling the sea to scoop out soft rock behind. Portland limestone stands fast on the seaward side, but once breached, the Purbeck limestone and Wealden Beds are more quickly eroded. There are bonuses close by – the Lulworth Crumple (rocks visibly folded) at Stair Hole; the Fossil Forest at Durdle Door. At Lulworth, the grass-topped white cliffs are crossed by white footpaths and little terraces of sheep tracks. From on high the picture of a safe haven is complete and the reasons for settlement obvious to the eye.

No doubt mariners along the north Cornwall coast learn quickly to distinguish Hells Mouth from Hudder Cove, and coastal footpath walkers head back to sandy Porthmeor and Treen Coves, Veor Cove or Pendour. Piskies Cove and Folly Cove beg further investigation. Cornwall shows well the difference between an open bay and a cove – a tiny inlet, often lined with sand, part of a complicated, varied coastline. Redshin Cove, just south of Berwick-upon-Tweed in Northumberland, is one of the very few in the north of England.

DEEZES

On the shingle beach – the Stade – at Hastings in Sussex a unique collection of three-storey weather-boarded huts squeeze together in front of the high sandstone cliffs.

Used to store fishing nets, rope and other tackle, they are known locally as deezes, a dialect word suggesting herring were originally dried here. The 45 remaining tarred sheds, some dating back to the sixteenth and seventeenth centuries, are constructed with diagonal bracing, the upper floors reached from inside by ladders nailed to the walls. Each

storey has an exterior door that opens outwards. Many deezes have been lost to fire but some have been rebuilt. They once extended much further along the beach, and were raised up on posts so the sea could wash beneath them. They may have Norse origins or connections with Spain via shipwrecked sailors.

In 1588 fishermen were charged a farthing a foot to lease land on Stonebeach, as it was known then. In the 1830s new council regulations stipulated that the huts should be no larger than eight foot square.

The Old Hastings Preservation Society has worked for thirty years to conserve these zany buildings for the fishermen – about forty boats still fish from here. Now they are a tourist attraction and no doubt the pressure will be on to turn them into pied-à-terres – as has happened to the old fishermen's huts at Whitstable, Kent. In Yorkshire flocks of green fishermen's huts were common from Redcar to Skinningrove, and the Northumberland coast has not only kipper smokeries but also old, upturned boats, tarred and doored for gear storage.

Hastings, Sussex.

ESTUARIES

We may associate the Tyne with fine bridges and a once-defining ship-building industry, the Tees with a twinkling and smelly chemical complex, the Humber with industry and latterly great fishing fleets, the Wash with open skies, the Thames with trade and commerce, the Blackwater with sailing, the Severn with its bore, the Mersey with songs and Morecambe Bay with a voracious running tide, but all of them are distinguished by being complex places in constant flux. These were the Saxon and Viking motorways, offering fast access inland. Where deep water is available, as in Southampton Water in Hampshire, they remain the points of entry for the heavy liquids that drive our economy.

Created where rivers run into the sea, our estuaries are tidal, offering a mosaic of challenges and opportunities for us and for wildlife. Some offer deep water, others are edged by salt marshes and rich mud-flats. They provide vital nurseries for many inshore marine fish, such as flounder, golden grey and thin-lipped mullets, sea trout and sea lamprey. Morecambe Bay, the Humber, Maplin Sands, the Ribble and Dee estuaries are key feeding grounds for wildfowl and waders, offering worms, shrimps and shellfish.

Likewise the Wash, fed by the rivers Nene, Ouse, Welland and Witham, extends over sand- and mud banks carved by intricately branching channels to more than 250 square miles, despite the massive drainage of the Fens. It supports huge populations of invertebrates and, in the south, brittle-stars and starfish. Eel grass is concentrated around the mouth of the Welland, where widgeon, teal, shelduck and mallard dominate. Enteromorpha, a type of algae, grows on the Wash flats, with huge flocks of knot, dunlin, curlew and oystercatcher as well as redshank, sanderling, bar-tailed godwit and grey and ringed plovers. Migrants add to the numbers. The sandbanks of the Nene, Ouse and Welland mouths attract common seals in quantity and some grey seals, too. In

the South West, at the Exe estuary, spoonbills and avocets are among the annual visitors.

Including the four shared with Scotland and Wales, England has 81 estuaries. They form our largest coastal habitat, one-fifth of Europe's Atlantic and North Sea tidal inlets. About a third of the estuarine surface has become dry land since Roman times, and much that remains is under pressure from port developments and industrial expansion. Chemicals and waste released into rivers accumulate in the estuarine sediment, risking long-lasting contamination. Rising sea levels compound the problems. For all these reasons, estuaries are among our most threatened maritime habitats.

FISH & CHIPS

The British devoured around three hundred million portions in 1999, sixty thousand tonnes of fish and half a million potatoes – more than ten per cent of all the potatoes eaten in the country in a year.

As with so many things we hold to be specially English, fish and chips is just another example of historic cultural weaving. Potatoes, of course, came from the Americas with Sir Walter Raleigh. The Belgians claim

Southampton Water, Hamphire.

the invention of the chip – even though they famously eat it with mayonnaise – but it is as likely that the French first cut potatoes into thin pieces and fried them as *pommes frites*. During the next two hundred years chips became popular in England, sold in Irish 'potato shops'.

In 1860 Joseph Malin opened a shop in Cleveland Street, Bow, east London, combining Franco-Belgic-Irish chips with fish fried in a style popularised by Portuguese Jews. From there the 'traditional' fish and chip shop evolved. Trade boomed as the new steam ships increased fishing productivity and the railways took advantage of developments in ice storage, bringing fresher fish from Grimsby, Fleetwood, Hull and Scotland to London.

As industrial workers gained a little disposable income, fish and chips became a staple, one of the few meals that working people could afford to buy ready-cooked and ready to eat. This was true well into the 1950s. Harry Ramsden opened the first sit-down chip restaurant in a hut at Guiseley near Leeds in 1928. Different regions had their preferences: hake in Lancashire, haddock in Yorkshire, dogfish or rock salmon in the North East. Laurie Fricker reports that in Glastonbury, Somerset you can have fish and chips served with cider.

Once paid holidays became the norm, industrial workers went to the seaside resorts and wanted the food they could buy at home. The resorts met demand by becoming increasingly synonymous with fried fish. To this day, according to statistics compiled by the National Federation of Fish Friers (NFFF), more than a third of the population *'believes that Blackpool serves the best fish and chips in the country'*. Food writer Tony Mudd is clear: *'the seaside is the best place to eat fish and chips. The fish is likely to have come straight from the sea, and the smell of chips will add to that holiday feeling.'* Among his favourites are the fish shop in Aldeburgh, Suffolk, Bill's Fish Bar in Cullercoats, Northumberland and Maddy's Chippy and Restaurant in Ilfracombe, Devon, where a fish and chip meal can be followed by apple and blackberry pie with custard.

Cod is by far the most popular fish, taking more than 61 per cent of

the chip-shop market, with haddock, plaice and whiting trailing behind. Some places, such as Seniors in Blackpool, offer more unusual varieties, including skate, John Dory, red snapper and black bream. These figures could be overturned, however, if the dramatic depletion of cod stocks around our shores during recent decades is not addressed. Its disappearance from chip-shop menus might be as much a necessary measure for saving it as a symptom of its decline.

For the chips, potatoes with a low-sugar, high-starch content are preferable. Maris Piper has been a favourite since its introduction in 1964, but Record is the industry standard. Crown, Cara, Dunbar Standard, Kestrel, Desiree, Pentland Squire, Pentland Dells and Idaho Russets have all been suggested as good chip spuds. James Leith summed up the type of potato essential for chipping: '*largish tuber, a high dry-matter content (that means it soaks up less oil) and a pale golden-finished colour*'.

At their peak in the 1920s, there were around 35,000 chip shops in Britain. In 2004 there were still nearly 8,600, far outstripping the seemingly ubiquitous burger bar by eight to one. The NFFF rewards the best with an annual award; recent winners have included the Brownsover Fish Bar in Rugby, Warwickshire, Bizzie Lizzies in Skipton, Yorkshire, The Halfway Fish Bar in Poole, Dorset and the Elite Fish Bar in Ruskington, Lincolnshire.

FOG & MIST

Clouds sometimes have to learn how to fly. They sit quite quiet or swirl a little, but keep contact with the ground. Mist is simply water droplets, too small to fall, impeding the view. It evokes a more benign, poetic

Wareham, Dorset.

outlook than fog, which is denser, cutting visibility to below a thousand metres. Inland fog is more likely in autumn and winter, especially after cold, clear nights. Sea fogs happen most often in spring and summer, when warmer air over a cooler sea brings the water vapour down to the dew point.

Fog changes our view of the world, literally and psychologically. Looking out from our hill town of Shaftesbury, it is not unusual to catch an early mist in Dorset's Blackmore Vale; on sharp winter's mornings this may lap like a sea around the 'islands' of Duncliffe, Melbury and Hambledon and at the 'shores' of Bulbarrow and far Rampisham.

Sometimes the clouds sit on the hilltops and threaten Marnhull and the other river Stour villages with rain:

> *If Duncliffe Wood be fair and clear,*
> *You Stour Boys need have no fear.*
> *But if Duncliffe Wood do wear its cap,*
> *You Marn'll folk watch out for that.*

In Sussex it runs: '*When Firle Hill and Long Man has a cap, We in the valley gets a drap.*' In Devon and Cornwall a wet hill fog goes by the name of mizzle. The Trent valley is naturally one of the foggiest places in England and this, together with the chemical reaction of fog with coal smoke, caused exceptionally severe smogs in the 1950s and 1960s.

Coal was understood to cause air pollution even in the thirteenth century. By 1661 John Evelyn had written in *Fumifugium* of the '*Hellish and dismal cloud of sea-coale*' that shrouded London and recommended banning trades that used it from the city. By 1800 a murky miasma along the Thames was known as a London Particular:

> *I asked him whether there was a great fire anywhere? For the streets were so full of dense brown smoke that scarcely anything was to be seen.*
> *'O dear no, miss,' he said. 'This is a London particular.'*

> *I had never heard of such a thing.*
> *'A fog, miss,' said the young gentleman.*
> *'O indeed!' said I.*

CHARLES DICKENS, from *Bleak House*

Its tendency to hug the docks was necessary to the plot of many a Sherlock Holmes mystery. By the mid-twentieth century this had evolved into the full pea-souper, tasting, as well as appearing, thick and greeny yellow. It killed people. The Great Smog in London, trapped by an inversion that lasted from 5 to 9 December 1952, led directly to the Clean Air Act of 1956 after at least four thousand people died. In the early 1960s east Londoners received thirty per cent less sunshine in winter than those who lived in the countryside around; now they receive about the same. While smogs seem to have been contained, many oil-derived pollutants make today's city air just as dangerous, but less visibly so.

If fog on land is disorientating and dangerous, imagine fog at sea, resting on the waves. The long, low moans of the diaphone foghorn on the lighthouse at Portland Bill, Dorset, sounding night and day, are viscerally registered. The Humber in fog used to be full of sounds, including the whoop-whoop-whoop of small boats seeming to dare the big vessels to play tag. '*You don't hear foghorns very often now, as all the boats have radar,*' Katrina Porteous writes of Northumberland. '*I loved the mournful sound of the one on Longstone. Further down the coast (on Coquet Island off Amble) there was "the Coquet Gun". The old men used to speak of "a thick" coming in. They seemed to use this word both for summer and winter fog, and both as a noun and an adjective. They used some lovely metaphors: thick as tar, thick as a hedge, thick as glaur (mud).*' In the North East, rook or roaky fogs tend to be thick, perhaps related to one of the nicknames for Edinburgh, Auld Reekie.

In the economical litany of the Shipping Forecast, after sea area, wind direction/speed and precipitation, comes visibility: '*moderate with fog patches, becoming good*'; or, the best punctuation of all, simply '*good*'.

FRETS

In Yorkshire, Durham and Northumberland the fret is a summer mist that occurs at the coast with moist air brought in on an easterly wind (and sometimes the tide). It is a frustrating phenomenon, being sometimes just tens of feet thick and a few hundred yards wide while just over the hill the day is beautiful. Villagers in Staithes, Yorkshire, with the arts group Blaize, captured its stealth:

> *From Eight Bells and Gun Gutter*
> *Broom Hill and Lining Garth*
> *Beck Side and Laverick Doorstones*
> *Old Stubble to Barber's Yard*
> *Up Slippery Hill to the Barras*
> *Through Dog Loup up from the Staithe*
> *The fret's creeping in from the harbour*
> *As the tide brings it on the wave*

The Scots call it the haar; in Scarborough, Yorkshire people know it as the sea roke. Local people and meteorologists have noticed that during the past twenty years frets have become less frequent because of the decrease in summer easterly winds, but the summer of 2004 seemed to bring a resurgence.

In north Norfolk the summer fret creates the best conditions for growing premium barley for malting. On the Isle of Wight the fret will occasionally creep in from the sea while cloud sits on the downs, leaving in between an extraordinary stratum of clear air with a view of both.

FUNICULAR RAILWAYS

Synonymous with 'cliff railways', as they are usually raised and lowered up and down an incline by cable (*funis* is Latin for rope), funicular railways appeared in the new seaside resorts in the nineteenth century. The earliest were on the rocky cliffs of Scarborough and Saltburn in Yorkshire. The latter, still working, extended to a pier at the foot of the cliff to make direct connections with pleasure boats. Scarborough's opened at South Cliff in 1884 and is still running, from the foreshore up 284 feet to the Esplanade.

Although many now run on electricity and diesel, such as the West Cliff lift at Hastings in Sussex, Scarborough's still depends on the water-balance principle. Both cars incorporate a water tank. Filling the tank of the car at the top makes it descend, pulling the lower one up. The lowered car discharges its load, while water is added at the top to continue the cycle.

The idea quickly spread. The famous railway linking Lynton and Lynmouth in Devon – the longest in the country – also uses the water-balance process. Without the funicular the two communities would still be wedged apart, the only link being a steeply twisting road. Southend in Essex and Torquay in Devon have them; Bournemouth in Hampshire has three; Folkestone in Kent, sadly, retains only one of three, although it has four tracks.

Inland, the Shipley Glen Tramway in Yorkshire gives visitors to Saltaire a lift up to the moors above, and Bridgnorth's Castle Hill tramway in Shropshire has ferried passengers between High and Low Town since 1891.

Saltburn, Yorkshire.

The last of the 'classic era' funicular railways to be built in England was at Fisherman's Walk in Pokesdown, Bournemouth, which is still active; since the 1980s several have appeared in theme parks.

GANSEYS

Guernsey and Jersey are well known for their cattle, but have no history of sheep farming. So how did they give us the blue woollen sweaters and generic names of gansey and jersey? Apparently Sir Walter Raleigh, Governor of Jersey in the early 1600s, initiated links between Newfoundland and the islands, which built a trade of building ships and making garments for seamen on imported wool. Guernseys are typically deep blue, while jerseys may be of other colours, too.

Seamen and especially fishermen around the north-east coast of England had a tradition of wearing sealskin that was gradually superseded by thick, knitted ganseys, which are virtually waterproof. The patterns belonging to different fishing families have passed down through generations. A book published by Tyne and Wear County Council Museums explains: *'They were knitted by eye, without a written pattern. Many of the designs incorporated in them had symbolic meaning. It is sometimes maintained that patterns were unique to particular villages or that it was possible to identify the origin of a drowned fisherman from the pattern of his gansey. While it was true that a fisherman's wife might be able to identify her own work, patterns were not unique, but were passed between villages, especially through marriage.'*

The comings and goings of Scots fishermen also ensured that patterns informed one another up and down the east coast. Many had the initials of the wearer knitted in. The stitches or *masks* (a Viking/Norwegian word) have particular names: zigzags were named after the steep paths winding up the cliffs; marriage lines or 'ups and downs' were a double zigzag; rope/cable, net or herring masks were stitches used in Flamborough, Yorkshire; double and single moss stitches were called sand and

Patrington & Withernsea, Yorkshire.

Filey, Yorkshire.

shingle; a double plait was print o'the hoof – like hoof marks in the sand; triple sea wave came from Northumberland; rig and fur, from Runswick Bay and Staithes in Yorkshire, was named after ridge and furrow fields.

Not until Gladys Thompson started to 'collect' the patterns in the 1930s were they written down. '*When I first remember Filey, every doorway in the old town held a knitter, in a black or coloured sunbonnet, with their needles flicking in and out so quickly it was impossible to follow their movements.*' Although some patterns are known by town or village, from Whitby, Scarborough and Staithes in Yorkshire to Craster in Northumberland, others carry the knitter's name – Mrs Foster from Withernsea, Betty Martin from Filey, Miss Ester Rutter from Seahouses, Mrs Rowe from Newbiggin.

Worked on five needles with the sleeves included, ganseys have no seams. Most of the ganseys of Yorkshire, Durham and Northumberland are dark blue, but in Amble on the river Coquet in Northumberland different colours are worn: grey for summer, blue for winter and black on Sundays and for funerals.

The tradition is dying, some say because the knitters can no longer get 'wassit' or fivefold (ply) double worsted of the quality needed.

GRAZING MARSHES

Marshes remain shifting, uncertain, often forbidding places. In Dickens's *Great Expectations*, Pip describes the moment he became aware that '*the dark flat wilderness beyond the churchyard, intersected with dikes and mounds and gates, with scattered cattle feeding on it, was the marshes; and that the low leaden line beyond was the river; and that the distant savage lair from which the wind was rushing was the sea*'.

Most often along the coast, marshes are watery lands, drained and defined by networks of dykes and protected from flooding by earthen walls or embankments. On rich clay and silt soils, rather than the peat-based fens, they offer valuable agricultural land, providing good pasture or even arable land. Here the dykes may have been first dug in late Saxon or medieval times. Reclamation from the sea has been achieved over centuries and plagued by setbacks, as land was lost as well as gained.

Marshes are a feature of the South and East and include the marshland of Lincolnshire, the Essex marshes, the Suffolk Sandlings and, in the Norfolk Broads, the wide expanse of the Halvergate marshes. Once a great estuary into which the rivers Bure, Yare and Waveney flowed, they are cut off from sight or sound of the sea and peppered with the ruins of brick tower mills, drainage schemes dating from the eighteenth century. Pollarded willows, cut low to withstand the wind, form close-set lines along the roads.

The marshes of north Kent still have a wild, windy and remote air, despite the oil refineries, paper mills and power stations on the skyline. In south Kent lies Romney Marsh, a vast stretch of windswept flatland scattered with houses and villages. Arable fields sometimes run up to the sea wall. Traces remain of the dense network of medieval dykes, and surrounding fields each amount to just two or three acres.

In Cumberland, along the Solway Firth, coastal grassland, known as merse, is dominated by bents and fescues, with autumn hawkbit, soft rush, Yorkshire fog and white clover. It provides fine grazing for sheep and is often colonised by gorse, altering the open character of the landscape.

Inland, grazing marshes once extended along many lowland rivers. In Sussex they are known as brooks, such as the Lewes Brooks and Malling Brooks in the Ouse valley, and Pulborough Brooks, now a Royal Society for the Protection of Birds reserve, on the Arun.

The intensification of coastal developments and agriculture has significantly reduced grazing marshland, now estimated to stand at less than half a million acres. Two-thirds of the Essex marshland and half of Romney Marsh were lost as grazing marsh between the 1930s and the 1980s. What remains is drying out and suffering nutrient overload from fertilisers. Only some twelve thousand acres of unimproved grassland remain, with a spread of native plant species and wetland breeding birds, such as lapwing, snipe and curlew, as well as overwintering flocks of Bewick's and whooper swans.

HARBOURS

Where sheltered havens do not naturally exist, we have conspired to build them. The shapes of harbours tell us much about the need for protection from winds and waves, tidal movements, the volatility of rivers and the problems of silting and longshore drift.

The rias of the South West offer natural anchorage out of the Atlantic weather, but elsewhere breakwaters, piers and quays create shelter, famously at Lyme Regis in Dorset, with its protective arm of the Cobb. Small stone harbours nestle into coves along the rocky coasts of Devon and Cornwall. The fishing village of Mevagissey in Cornwall has an inner and an outer harbour, both embraced by walls. The harbours of Shoreham, Sussex and Great Yarmouth, Norfolk, which take advantage of long, deflected estuaries, need constant dredging. Staithes, Yorkshire cowers

Mevagissey, Cornwall.

Dover, Kent.

Whitehaven, Cumberland.

Blyth, Northumberland.

Lowestoft, Suffolk.

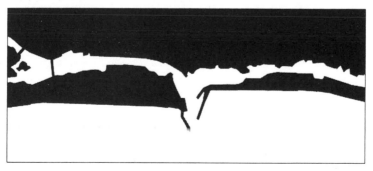

Shoreham, Sussex.

into the steep ravine behind its breakwaters and, like so many small harbours, it dries at low tide. By contrast, Whitehaven in Cumberland offers 25 acres of water behind lock gates.

Small harbours continue their decline as fishing and trading patterns change. Leisure boating and tourism are moving in. At Brighton the artificial harbour at Black Rock is one of the biggest marina developments in Europe.

HARDS

A hard, often simply and anciently constructed, is a firm edge of stone, gravel or concrete along a river or seaside foreshore. Small ferries, boat builders, fishermen and commercial adventurers all need small-scale landing and launching places, together with myriad recreation seekers, from dinghy sailors to anglers, who want to reach the water. But rights of access to the edges of rivers and the sea have dwindled, together with those of our footpaths and commons.

Hithes, staithes, quays, steps and stairs all offer possibilities. Along the Hampshire coast the county council has identified seventy public slipways or hards and nine beach launching areas. The Bursledon Rights of Way Group is fighting for continued access to the river Hamble, where commercial activity has given way to recreational use and encroachment by developers presses. Similarly, along the river Thames, Kim Wilkie has counted more than forty slipways from Hampton to Isleworth and many more landing stages.

ISLANDS

Although we add the words 'island' or 'isle' to Brownsea, Hilbre, Horsey, Mersea, Northey, Osea, Osney, Scilly, Sheppey and Walney, they are already implied in the Old English *eg* or Old Norse *ey*. Even in landbound Canvey in Essex, Ely in Cambridgeshire and Muchelney in Somerset, memories of plashy beginnings are embedded in the name.

Lundy means puffin island in Old Norse. Although only half a mile by three, it stands a proud granite beacon at four hundred feet high, with room for birds, flowers and lichens – the puffins for which it was named are few now. Its position in the Bristol Channel means that the pirate, the wrecker and the lighthouse (actually two) have a history here, but its modern role is as a retreat, bird colony, tourist haven and sheep farm. It is surrounded by the pioneering marine nature reserve of Europe, and more than a square mile of sea has also been designated the UK's first No Take Zone, meaning that no living thing can be fished or dredged-for here.

Around the island there are fine rocky reefs of coral and sponge, as well as magnificent kelp forests, with visiting basking sharks, resident seals and laid-back lobsters. The Lundy cabbage is unique to the island and plays sole host to a couple of flea beetles and a weevil found nowhere else. The meat of the Soay sheep that maintain the herbage is marketed with a Lundy label; there is also a Lundy stamp for your postcard home from this little piece of land, which was once owned, notwithstanding names such as the Devil's Slide and Devil's Limekiln, by the Heaven family, who bought it with money gained from Jamaican estates when the slaves were emancipated.

Tiny Steep Holm and Flat Holm, limestone outliers of the Mendips – one steep, one flat – lie further into the Bristol Channel. Holm is an Old Norse word for island.

The Isle of Wight is a giant in comparison, 23 by 13 miles. Flashing its chalk cliffs to the east and west, it enlivens the horizon from Portsmouth and Bournemouth. This island stands in the way of water striving to ebb and flow north and south, east and west, creating a unique double tide that is felt along the nearby coasts of Hampshire and Dorset. It interferes with the wind, too, making the Solent challenging for sailing.

The Isles of Scilly in Cornwall are made of defiant ancient granite confronting a ravaging ocean, an archipelago of rocks and lands so resilient that gales with a fetch of thousands of miles and ships at full throttle barely seem to graze their edges. Far out of sight of other land, the elements rule here. Yet things do change. Only four thousand years ago this was made up of fewer, bigger islands; sea level was lower and the tilting of the whole mass had not accelerated. Now the main islands are surrounded by drowned prehistoric fields and villages, as well as rocks and wrecks, hundreds of them – there are at least thirteen broken ships on the Crim Rocks to the west, and islets have warning names, such as Hellweathers, Roaring Ledge, Steeple Rock, The Hats and Ragged Island. Geoffrey Grigson apprehended it: '*The islands are raw and original in the whole, humanised only in the detail. The detail is rich, curious, coloured, varied and variegated … but it is the original which governs, the human which is incidental.*'

Hilbre, Little Hilbre and Little Eye form a broken rampart of long, low sandstone islands edging the Wirral in Cheshire, surrounded by miles of red tidal sands. The patterns of lugworm casts and rippled sand texture the hour-long walk across at low tide. Sea spleenwort and rock sea-lavender may be rare, but most surprising is to find bluebells among the thrift in early spring. The marshes and mud-flats, sands and sea make this a rich place for birds, resident and migrating, which in turn make this a place of birdwatchers and ringers; the bird observatory has been here since 1957.

The Great Whin Sill marches across the northern edge of England, standing in a high cliff as it meets the sea below Bamburgh castle in Northumberland. It reappears a couple of miles out as the dark Farne Islands, 28 pieces of dolerite, some disappearing under the tide, the larger

being coated in boulder clay and peaty soil. Puffins normally breed here in serious numbers, together with kittiwakes, guillemots and shags among the thirteen species that nest on different islands, but, as at Coquet Island further south, breeding is now erratic. Scientists fear a catastrophic fall in numbers as a result of rising temperature in the North Sea: it has increased by two degrees Celsius in twenty years, and sand eels are following plankton further north as the sea warms.

Coquet Island, off Amble in Northumberland, is for the birds. It has a lighthouse built on a monastic outpost of Tynemouth Priory. St Cuthbert spent time here as well as living in solitude on Inner Farne, where he tried to stop the plundering of the eider duck – it has since locally been named after him as Cuddy's duck. Both he and St Aidan before him were also associated with Lindisfarne, or Holy Island, making it a place of pilgrimage and retreat for 1,300 years. The most pious still cross the tidal causeway on foot, overtaken by drivers careful to note the tide tables.

Islands that can be reached at low tide have a certain magic. St Nicholas at Wade in Kent stands beside the old wading place to the Isle of Thanet, and just to the north is Plumpudding Island. St Michael's Mount in Cornwall rises three hundred feet, with a zigzag track to a medieval priory, fortified church, cottages and shops. This high-tide island, a dramatic landmark all along the south Cornish coast, is reached by boat or causeway from Marazion. On the north coast Tintagel, with its tales of Merlin and King Arthur, has become an island since the sea severed its natural arch.

JET

Akin to coal, though much lighter in weight, jet is a fossilised wood from a Jurassic relative of the monkey-puzzle tree. Like amber, a tree resin, it is easily shaped and polished and feels warm to the touch. Rubbed on wool or silk it soon picks up a static electrical charge. The intensity of its blackness is also remarkable. These must be some of the reasons why it was highly prized by prehistoric people – jet beads have been found in high-status Bronze-Age burials near the Sussex coast.

The best hard jet in England comes from around Whitby in north Yorkshire, where miners soon learned that a particular sort of ammonite fossil was a reliable indicator of jet-bearing rock. In its heyday in the 1870s the industry employed three hundred men, including craftsmen who carved the jet into the elaborate ornaments and mourning jewellery beloved of the Victorians. Today the seaside resort supports a thriving market in both antique jet and new craftwork, with stiff competition to find rough jet in the cliffs or on the beach after winter storms.

KIPPERS

No kipper ever swam in the seas. Kippering is a curing and smoking process, which transforms a humble herring into something that cookery writer Jane Grigson justly described as *'one of this country's worthy contributions to fine food'*.

The English kipper is a product of the North East. John Woodger of Seahouses in Northumberland is credited with the invention of kippered herring in the 1840s, although it is a far from positive identification. The word itself seems to derive from the Dutch *küpper*, 'to spawn', and refers to the end-of-season salmon, which was not wasted if it was split and smoked. The North East has always been emotionally closer to the Netherlands and Scandinavia, where herrings are practically a staple (even IKEA's food halls demonstrate it). Woodger marketed the 'Newcastle kipper' in the markets of London and, thanks to railways and fridges, they are coming still.

Think of them and two places immediately spring to mind: Craster in Northumberland, where the Robson family's smokery has been hard at work since the 1850s; and Whitby in Yorkshire, where the Gothic associations with Bram Stoker are only enhanced by the conjoining in the narrow Victorian streets of the sea mist and the aromatic smoke from Willy Fortune's smokehouse.

Further south in Norfolk, Great Yarmouth's connection with the fish was so important (although its main stock-in-trade was the bloater – whole, salted, cold-smoked herring – rather than the kipper) that three herrings appear on the town's coat of arms. Woodger extended his empire to Yarmouth to use local fish and, as in North Shields, utilised the talents of Scots women, who migrated with the trade and became known as 'herring lassies'.

The kippering process is straightforward. Herrings are split and gutted, cleaned, salted, then hung on wooden poles or 'tenter-sticks' from metal hooks. For these authentic smokeries there are no dyes or impatiently speedy throughput. At Robson's the kippers are hung for up to fourteen hours above fires of whitewood shavings topped with oak sawdust. Fortune's smokes them for up to thirty hours, then sells them in pairs.

In spite of occasional threats from would-be legislators, there are still a few other producers using traditional methods, including Swallows of

Seahouses. Like the others they have to rely on Scottish and Icelandic herring, the fish being peculiarly fickle geographically. The shoals of the nineteenth century, in Bill Weeks's words, *'would turn the sea's surface to quicksilver'*. But the herrings vanished as mysteriously as they came and, inevitably, took the local trade with them. The last were landed at Whitby in the 1970s. North Sea herring fishing was banned in 1977 in the hope that the stocks would be re-established.

LAGOONS

Of the hundred lagoons around the English coast, a quarter are in Hampshire, but the largest is in Dorset. Here, the Fleet shelters behind Chesil Bank and is home to the largest mute swan colony in the UK. The name 'fleet' recurs along the Essex coast, as in Broad, Besom, Mersea and Tollesbury Fleets. Suffolk has many little rivers more or less frustrated in their approach to the sea by sandbars; here they are called broads. Just south of Kessingland lie Benacre, Covehithe and Easton Broads.

Lagoons vary in salinity; some are tidal. The shingle bar at Slapton Ley in south Devon holds back a virtually freshwater lake. The reeds here welcome clouds of roosting starlings in winter. Most lagoons attract different waders and wildfowl, but less mobile creatures have to be specialised to cope with an uncertain saline content. Delicate stoneworts, the lagoon sand shrimp and the starlet sea anemone may be found. The trembling sea mat is found in only one Cornish lagoon – Swanpool, near Falmouth.

LIDOS

Poor fitness of conscripts in the First World War prompted a national drive for health improvement. Open-air swimming caught the public imagination and, from the 1920s, pools appeared from London to Ilkley in Yorkshire, including tidal pools, as at Shoalstone in Brixham, Devon and Walpole Bay at Cliftonville, Margate, Kent. These were rendered exotic by being called lidos, after the Italian word for beach and, more directly, referring to the municipal bathing area in Venice.

Often grandly set within Art Deco complexes, they proved expensive to maintain, and few survive. Many closed during the 1980s and 1990s, including those at Hackney in east London, Stoke-on-Trent in Staffordshire, New Brighton in Cheshire and Alfreton in Derbyshire. The Olympic-sized lido built using miners' contributions at Murton Colliery in Durham – once the only pool of its size between Sheffield and Edinburgh – was closed with the pit in 1991 and demolished because the council would not take it on.

Campaigns by local people and the Twentieth Century Society have led to increased recognition and funding. Brockwell near Brixton, south London, built in 1937, was rescued from near dereliction in the 1990s, as was Ilkley, with its Art Deco café, fountain and startling view over the moors. Listed lidos include Saltdean near Brighton in Sussex and the tidal pool at Penzance in Cornwall, with its grand terraces. Tinside at Plymouth was restored and re-opened as part of the city's waterfront regeneration in 2003. The three pools at Tunnels Beach in Ilfracombe, Devon are being restored, one at a time. A new drive for health and developing technology may yet see a resurgence of the much-loved outdoor pool.

LIGHTHOUSES

Lighthouses have saved ships and inspired us. John Constable, Eric Ravilious and Virginia Woolf responded to their melancholy and constancy. Benedict Mason's musical composition *Lighthouses of England and Wales* (1991) orchestrates the pulses from forty lights. '*See hoo she*

Burnham-on-Sea, Somerset.

Dungeness, Kent.

Portland Bill, Dorset.

Smeaton's Tower, Plymouth Hoe, Devon.

flashes an' fades in the hush/A' the dark an' the sea,' wrote Katrina Porteous of Longstone Light in Northumberland, the scene of Grace Darling's heroism in 1838.

These slender, tapering, blinking columns are rich with the draw of the sea, like the four that have successively stood at Eddystone, fourteen miles from Plymouth, Devon since 1698. They come in many shapes and sizes. A boxy white building underpins Bamburgh's lantern in

Northumberland. Fleetwood's low light in Lancashire has ornate balconies above a classically pillared shelter. Watchet in Somerset has a small, red, hexagonal tower with a slate pagoda roof, rather like a tall pillar-box. Some are even inland: Weldon church in Northamptonshire doubled as a lighthouse guiding people through once treacherously dense woods.

Dover in Kent has its Roman Pharos ruins. Later the Church protected its trading interests by displaying warning lights on coastal chapels; some, like St Peter the Poor Fisherman in Revelstoke, Devon, were built solely for that purpose. St Nicholas at Ilfracombe in Devon is still illuminated. Local story has the fourteenth-century Pepper Pot (or Salt Cellar) at St Catherine's Point on the Isle of Wight built in penance after shipwrecked goods belonging to the Church were plundered.

Private ownership was the lucrative norm. Trinity House was formed to represent mariners' interests, building its first lighthouse at Lowestoft, Suffolk in 1609 and, over time, buying out the others. Sometimes the payments benefited the community. The Reverend David Davies was the driving force behind the wooden box on stilts that still stands at Burnham-on-Sea, Somerset. The funds received bought the town's bath house, esplanade and the hamlet of Daviesville.

Of the 72 active lighthouses in England in 2004, all are now automated and many have lost their voices. The last to have residents, until 1998, was North Foreland, Kent. Dungeness, Kent gained a sleek modern lighthouse in 1961, floodlit to be more visible to night shipping and migrating birds. The black-painted Old Light came up for sale in 2005 for £150,000. The Needles and Bishop Rock (Isles of Scilly) lights are now truncated by the addition of helicopter landing pads. Many, such as Lundy South, are solar-powered. Some, like the Gothic Belle Tout, near Beachy Head in Sussex, are private houses. Others, including Lundy Old Light and Trevose, near Padstow in Cornwall, have become holiday homes.

Lighthouses are usually white with black or red stripes to stand out against sky, land or cliffs. They have become local icons and tourist magnets. The Isles of Scilly council has incorporated Bishop Rock into its new island flag.

LINKS

The coastal sand-dunes found along the Northumberland coast are known as links. Where they are not held together by marram grass or sheep-trimmed turf, the wind will create natural bunkers, making it easy to see how they, or rather their Scottish counterparts, gave birth to golf.

Lindisfarne, Ross, Bamburgh, Beadnell, Embleton, Alnmouth and Warkworth all have extensive links. Newton Links has for more than twenty years fallen under the gaze of Phil Gates, who says the dunes have '*a wonderful natural economy – for example, the scarlet and black sexton beetles that serve as gravediggers for dead birds and mammals by excavating the sand under the corpse and then laying their eggs in the underground larder*'. With common blue, small copper and wall butterflies, harebells, lizards, dragonflies and all manner of sea and land birds, the links are just holding their own against modern golf-courses, which, in their attempt to emulate, only reduce the richness.

LOST VILLAGES

On the east coast the sea has been eating soft land and settlements with relish. It transports debris along the coast and drops it, to make new land, fill in harbours and wreck ships. The Yorkshire coast of Holderness suffers losses of four to seven feet a year, with occasional lurches of twenty feet in a day. The cliffs may reach above eighty feet in height, but the boulder clay is no match for storm waves.

In 1786 one J. Tuke made a ghostly map of places '*washed away by the sea*' – Hartburn, Kilham, Hyde, Hornsea Burton, Aldbrough, ancient

Withernsea and Frismarsh. Before him, in 1360, the *Liber Melsae* mentions the loss of Hotton, Northorpe, Dymitton and Out Newton. We can add Sunthorpe, the old port of Hornsea, Seathorne or Owthorne, and Atwick. The mobility of Spurn, a series of sand and shingle banks extending into the Humber estuary, has seen the loss of Ravensrodd, built in the mid-thirteenth century and lost within a hundred years.

In Suffolk, Dunwich was a busy market town at the start of the thirteenth century, failing by the end of it. House after house, church after church '*yielded to the impetuosity of the billows breaking against and undermining the foot of the precipices*', a story told time after time in guide books. The port and ten churches have been lost. The succession of artists drawn to the drama included Turner, who captured the Church of All Saints, perched and vulnerable; it fell finally in 1912.

Stories, folktales, archaeological evidence and historical records mount up. Beyond the pier at Southend, Essex lies Milton; sandbanks now submerged off the Kent coast perhaps once supported fishermen's huts; St Enodoc's Church in Cornwall may be a remnant of a village overtaken by sand; Shotwick in Cheshire was lost, though the church remains, defended by reclaimed land of the Wirral.

Coastal villages are not the only casualties. In Gloucestershire the village of Charlton was flattened under Filton airfield, extended for the ill-fated Brabazon airliner in the late 1940s; reservoir building in Yorkshire claimed West End and Timble; Derwent and Ashopton were swallowed by the Ladybower Dam in Derbyshire, and Mardale by Haweswater in Westmorland. Low rainfall in 2003 revealed Mardale's streets and walls, adding to the distress of local people and the appeal for sightseers.

The Celtic lost land of Lyonesse had been written of by Richard Carew in the Survey of Cornwall 1602 as the birth place of King Arthur. Camden's *Britannia* linked it with Lethowsow or the Seven Stones between the Isles of Scilly and Land's End. Local stories have echoes of the Breton tale of Kêr-Is, the Welsh story of Bottom Cantred and, indeed,

Atlantis. The Isles of Scilly have themselves lost land and buildings since Roman times, when it is possible that isles were joined – partly submerged hut circles, walls and burial chambers attest to this. But the story of Lyonesse – '*A land of old upheaven from the abyss/By fire, to sink into the abyss again*' (Tennyson) – recounts the loss of the City of Lions (Carlyon), much good land and 140 churches.

The sea will have its way and scientists are now acknowledging this by encouraging 'managed realignment'. In the process the north Norfolk coast, for example, will be constantly redrawn, with villages such as Bacton, Mundesley, Ostend and Walcott slipping away during the next century. The removal of millions of tons of aggregate from the seabed off the coast, to be sold to Holland and Belgium to shore up their own coastal defences, does not help and leaves residents apoplectic.

Tim O'Riordan, professor of environmental sciences at UEA, says: '*Building sea walls on a mobile and eroding coast is ultimately a waste of time and money. Where there are major communities and installations at stake we may have no other choice but to try to defend as best we can. Where there is a highly dynamic beach and rapidly eroding cliffs, such works may defend odd properties, but they destroy coastlines. A mobile seashore will protect more by letting nature replenish the beaches. I care about the fate of endangered villages, and am trying to use the new planning frameworks to create sustainable villages alongside redesigned coastlines, with the help of the residents and newcomers. This process will take ten to fifty years to complete, but new communities will evolve out of danger.*'

MARTELLO TOWERS

Martello towers are particular to the south and east coasts, built, all in a rush, between 1805 and 1812 to protect these shores from Napoleon's advances. Each was topped by a large gun, more terrifying to ships trying to land men than the one used in performances of Tchaikovsky's symphony. Inspired by a defensive tower that repulsed our navy at Mortella,

Corsica, these small sea batteries were built mainly of brick and rendered, with walls up to thirteen feet thick towards the sea and five feet to landward. Some had dry moats. A door more than halfway up the thirty-feet-high battered walls was reached by a removable ladder.

Of the original 74 in the South, 29 can be found between Folkestone in Kent and Seaford in Sussex. They are elliptical in shape, compared with the slightly later ovoid plan of the eighteen (out of 27) up the coast of East Anglia, from St Osyth Stone in Essex to Aldeburgh in Suffolk, where a four-gun, quatrefoil tower survives. Three Redoubts, which were more complicated and carried ten guns, were built; two can still be seen at Eastbourne in Sussex and Dymchurch in Kent, the latter used by the army. A way beyond it is Martello tower number nineteen; raided finally by the sea in 1975, it lies in a scrambled heap, the most challenging of beach sculptures. Tower number fifteen, near Hythe in Kent, leans not far from number fourteen, both sturdy landmarks, for the moment. Elsewhere, towers are lived in or have become museums and cafés, having been sold by the Ministry of Defence for one pound or more.

NATTERJACK TOADS

The natterjack toad is the rarest of our amphibians, partly because of its exacting living demands, and we have not made its life easy. It is a creature of sand-dunes and sandy heaths, requiring temporary, seasonally flooded, shallow, unshaded pools in which to spawn, short turf in which to forage and sand to burrow in for hibernation. It spawns later than the common toad and frog, usually in April to June, when the pools have had a chance to warm up, and because of the danger of the pools drying out, the tadpoles develop more quickly than their amphibian cousins.

Night-time social croaking of the males is for the benefit of females at the spawning ponds in spring and can be heard a mile away on warm, still nights. On the Sefton coast, between the estuaries of the Ribble and the Mersey in Lancashire, the largest sand-dune system in England contains the greatest number of natterjack toads. They have probably lived here for nine and a half thousand years, which demands some respect. In 1838 they were noted as being 'in great abundance' in the dune systems around Ainsdale, where their vernacular names are Southport nightingale and Bootle organ. On the Surrey heathlands they were called the Thursley thrush. Other local names include Goldenbacks in Surrey, after their yellow stripe, Running Toad and Walking Toad in East Anglia, because of

Sefton coast, Lancashire.

their running gait, and natterjack 'nadder' in Lincolnshire, from the Old English, meaning 'to crawl'.

The natterjack toad was locally abundant on the heathlands of Surrey, East Anglia, Dorset and Hampshire and the dune systems of the Lancashire, Lincolnshire and other sandy coasts before twentieth-century incursions. Now only isolated populations remain and, to help its survival, English Nature is translocating toads to suitable habitats.

NOBBIES

Nobbies are found working the tidal waters from the Dee to the Solway Firth. They are carvel-built, of shallow draught, with a sharp bow adapted for negotiating shifting sands under sail or motor. The Morecambe Bay nobby was used for trawling for shrimp, although it is often called a prawner; it has a deck, open cockpit and often carried a stove, for boiling the catch while still fishing. Elegant under sail, it has been the inspiration for popular yacht designs; it now earns its keep as much from tourist trips as from shrimping.

'OBBY 'OSSES

Hobby-horses, for such is their refined title, could be ancient – they may have arrived with the Anglo-Saxons – but not until the fifteenth century do we find documentary evidence of their presence and activities. Two main 'breeds' exist: the tourney, or tournament, horse, in which a 'rider', often masked, protrudes above a skirted hoop that disguises not four but two legs; and the simpler mast, or pole, horse, in which a powerful head (sometimes a real horse's skull) sits on a pole with cloth concealing both pole and bearer.

In reviving the Hunting of the Earl of Rone, not performed between 1837 and the 1970s, Combe Martin in Devon has researched its own history and reinvented a powerful celebration. A hobby-horse and its company once more take a turn around the village on Ascension Day (now the first May bank holiday). The cast of characters comprises the Earl of Rone in a mask, with ship's biscuits in a string around his neck; a large hobby-horse with mappers – snapping jaws; a live donkey, also with a biscuit collar; a Fool with a besom; and a troop of grenadier guards (sojers) in red coats with (sort of) muskets.

At eventide five hundred villagers swell the ranks. They are led up to Lady's Wood, where all hunt for the Earl of Rone. Shots are fired, the Earl is caught and ignominiously made to ride the donkey with his face to its tail. Journeying towards the sea, incidents occur – each time volleys are fired, guards are praised, drums are beaten, lamentations take place – and the Fool raises the Earl from wounds or death. As the sun sets the players and the crowd reach the shore and, with a great crescendo, things happen in the sea. In the early nineteenth century '*licence and drunkenness*' then began, which led a rector to have all the costumes burned; the ceremony was suppressed in 1837.

Scraps of history may be intertwined with ancient ritual. In 1607 the Earl of Tyrone, escaping from Ireland after insurrection, was washed ashore, perhaps here or in France. Skimmity riding, being made to ride a donkey backwards to the sound of pans being clashed together, is an old form of rough punishment. In Rome the October horse, drowned each October, wore biscuits to symbolise the end of harvest.

Hobby-horses and other beasts take centre stage in many ancient customs. The horse mask is played out in spring not only in a few corners of England but, as Violet Alford found, in Austria, the Czech Republic, France, Poland, Slovakia and Switzerland.

In Minehead, Somerset there is luck in greeting and paying the hobby-horse that ventures out on May Day. Minehead has even customised the calendar: Warning Eve or Show Night is the local name for 30 April, when the Sailor's Horse first appears. He dances to his own tune in the streets as drum and melodeon are played by the 'sailors', who attend him. Before six o'clock on May morning the Sailor's Horse bows three times to the rising sun, then starts on his way. Chasing children, prancing precariously near the water's edge by the harbour, seeing off the Town Horse with his Gullivers 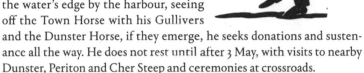 and the Dunster Horse, if they emerge, he seeks donations and sustenance all the way. He does not rest until after 3 May, with visits to nearby Dunster, Periton and Cher Steep and ceremonies at crossroads.

At the same time the equally robust Old Hoss and friends will be busy in Padstow on the north Cornish coast. At midnight all eighteen verses of the 'Night Song' are sung to rouse particular residents from their beds. All is then quiet until eight in the morning, when two children's 'osses appear and dance for an hour. At ten o'clock on May morning the Blue Ribbon horse emerges. At midday (eleven o'clock British Summer Time) the Old Hoss gets up to celebrate the first day of summer. All day long 'Day Song' alternates with 'Night Song', both of which begin:

> *Unite and unite and let us all unite,*
> *For summer is acome unto day,*
> *And whither we are going we will all unite,*
> *In the merry morning of May.*

Black, light on his feet and bold with the ladies, the Old Hoss dances and rampages. Accompanied by the Teaser and mayers dressed in white, he corners and envelops girls with his skirts to much shrieking. From time to time he dies and is revived. All the while the sound of drums and accordions accompanies the songs, shouts and screams. In neighbouring streets Blue Ribbon goes about his business and, in the evening, they meet at the maypole, which is topped with larch and flowers, to dance before being stabled until the next year.

Padstow claims these traditions have possible connections with ancient Britons and four thousand years of settlement in their place. The Minehead custom may have grown out of beating the bounds, or repelling Viking attacks, or a shipwreck involving a drowned cow – academics and residents muse and disagree.

Hooden horses are particular to east Kent. A carved horse head with a noisy, articulated lower jaw is affixed to a pole hung with hessian, which hides the performer. He is accompanied by a carter, a rider and a betsy (man as woman), who join him in a short play performed for money before Christmas – a time when work was short. After virtually dying out, hoodening had a resurgence in the 1950s. A new white horse, Invicta (after Kent's emblem), appeared and has joined the East Kent Morris Men. More hooden horses have appeared and, in 1998, three appeared together in one play. They can be seen between Whitstable and Folkestone.

The Wild Horse (or Hodening Horse) appears in Cheshire on All Saints' and All Souls' Days at the start of November. In Antrobus he accompanies a souling (St George) play around the pubs with his driver, dressed as huntsman. In Richmond, Yorkshire, T'Owd 'Oss appears on Christmas and New Year's Eves; this tradition is secretly passed on through families. Old Tup (a ram with similar tendencies to the 'obby 'oss) occasionally emerges where Derbyshire, Nottinghamshire and Yorkshire meet.

In Oxfordshire a brand-new gathering is taking root. The Banbury Hobby Horse Festival honours a nursery rhyme and reinforces the identity of the place. At the end of June Banbury welcomes many beasts to its streets to perform and dance, to race, to joust, to be admired. Accounts of the first few years suggest there is a lot of horsing about.

OYSTERS

Gin and gingerbread herald the start of the dredging season for the much-coveted oyster fishery near Colchester, Essex in September. The Mayor, Chief Executive and Town Sergeant, in civic robes, set out with forty guests on a sailing barge from Brightlingsea to the main oyster farming beds in the Pyefleet Channel by Mersea Island. The ancient Proclamation of 1256, which affirms Colchester's exclusive rights for time immemorial, is read and the fishery declared open. The Mayor drinks the Loyal Toast to the Queen with gin, followed by gingerbread, orders the first dredge to be made and has the honour of eating the first oyster. All are treated to an oyster lunch. A month later, on the eve of St Dennis's Day (21 October), four hundred guests indulge in an Oyster Feast at Colchester's Moot Hall.

Oyster fishing took place before the Romans built Colchester, where the Pyefleet Native thrived in the shallow creeks around the mouth of the Thames and in the estuaries of the rivers Colne, Crouch, Blackwater, Roach and along the Essex coast. The oysters were dredged – scraped off their beds – but conservation measures as early as 1577 prevented harvesting between Easter and Lammas, when the oysters were spawning (spatting). At its height in the 1860s the Colne Fishery produced about seven million oysters a year. Now the centre of the industry is Mersea Island, where Mersea Natives and Colchesters are sold from The Company Shed on the foreshore. Local fishermen are still lobbying to date to get Protected Geographical Indication status for Colchesters.

Until the 1860s oysters were the food of the poor. But the once-thriving industry was ruined by overfishing, propelled by railway links to Billingsgate Market in London. Then came polluted rivers and disease. Imported oysters brought with them the slipper limpet, American oyster-drill and the barnacle from the antipodes, creatures that harm or destroy oyster beds. The severe winters of 1947 and 1963, floods and toxic anti-fouling paints all added to their demise. Oysters have become scarce, a delicacy for the rich.

Whitstable Oyster Festival and Blessing of the Waters takes place around St James's Day, 25 July. The first catch of the season is blessed and presented to the Mayor, then paraded through the town, accompanied by the civic party, Shire horses, dray and musicians, before being delivered to restaurants, pubs and cafés. There is music, oysters for sale, boats to board and trips on sailing barges. The Men of Kent and Kentish Men present the annual Blessing of the Waters ceremony on Reeves Beach, and the festival ends with fireworks over the sea.

Present-day cultivation takes place from Suffolk to Cornwall. Native oyster grounds are still found in the estuaries of the Thames, Solent, Helford and Fal – on the Fal the oysters are dredged by the world's last sail-powered fishing fleet and the boats race one another at the annual Falmouth Oyster Festival in October. But none of the grounds recovered from the winter of 1963, which killed 95 per cent of stocks. A closed season protects native oysters while spawning, spatfall, which happens with the full moons between 14 May and 4 August.

PANTILES

Stacked up in composite heaps
Single Romans, Double Romans,
Triple Romans
Pan tiles, Finials, Triple Angulars,
Scallops, Clubs, Plain and Ziggurat
Weatherblock and Bargeboard
Waterbar and Hurricane, Fishscale and Homestead
Wineglass Paragon, Lockjaw and Marseille –
Acres of roof running wild, miles of tiles.

JAMES CROWDEN, from 'Bridgwater Reclaimed'

Pantiles are a celebration of baked clay and the subtle range of colours it can produce. Unlike flat, plain tiles they are S-shaped to interlock. With local variations, they give a furrowed appearance to roofs, rippled with alternate lines of light and shade.

The traditional areas for pantiles are those that traded with Holland in the seventeenth and eighteenth centuries: predominantly along the east coast from the Thames estuary to Scotland, around Bridgwater in Somerset and up the Bristol Channel. Bridgwater exported wool to the Netherlands and brought pantiles back; in the early eighteenth century companies began to make their own bricks and pantiles from local clay. They were sent up the Severn as far as Gloucester, down the Bristol Avon to the Vale of Pewsey in Wiltshire, and up the river Parrett into Somerset, where they gradually replaced thatch.

On the east coast pantile making began at places such as Tilbury, Essex (by a firm owned by Daniel Defoe) and Barton-upon-Humber. They were shipped up the Humber and Trent into Lincolnshire and Nottinghamshire, and up the Welland, Nene and Ouse. The coast of Northumberland, the Tees valley, the North York Moors and the Vale of York are traditional pantile-roof areas, as is the coast edging Essex, Suffolk, Norfolk (and Cambridgeshire), where they vary in colour from red in north Norfolk to brown in the south.

Pantiles were readily accepted because, although larger, fewer were needed. They overlap at each side, whereas plain tiles have to be two to three deep to keep out the rain. Less weight meant fewer roof timbers and a reduction in labour costs. They also enabled the pitch of the roof to be as low as thirty degrees, although when replacing thatch they were laid on roofs as steep as 55 degrees.

The S-shaped are the most common, but shapes vary, from the Essex flat-and-roll to the Bridgwater flat-and-two-rolls and the *'small-scale double-S, which gives a much more even overall ripple to the roof'*, described by John and Jane Penoyre.

Colours vary, from bright red in the Vale of York to brownish red in parts of Suffolk and a pale buff colour in Cambridgeshire. A speciality of Boston in Lincolnshire and north Norfolk, glazed black pantiles were imported into Hull in the seventeenth century from Holland – glazing gave them added strength and protection against frost. They were particularly admired by Richard Fortey, *'when they are combined with tar-washed sea cottages on the Norfolk coast'*, and by the Penoyres, who wrote that the *'shiny, black-glazed pantiles … look extremely well on flint buildings'*. Alec Clifton-Taylor remarked: *'When they reflect the sky they often appear dark blue.'*

There are few companies making pantiles today. After the Second World War volume house-builders preferred concrete tiles. The last Somerset tile makers disappeared in the 1950s, creating a thriving second-hand market in Bridgwater double romans for older properties in Bristol and surrounding areas. Sandtoft, a firm of tile makers based in Yorkshire and Humberside, still produces handmade and machine-made tiles and traditional pantiles, including the Bridgwater double roman and single roman.

PENNY HEDGE

Also known as Horngarth, Kightly believed that this could be *'the oldest surviving manorial custom in Britain'*. It involves the Hutton family, who rent farm land at Fylingdales near Whitby, Yorkshire, in an annual custom extraordinary in its persistence.

Complaints about excesses of wood being sold in 1315 seem to have led to the ritual, but by the time of the Dissolution abbots seem to have concocted a story, as Kightly wrote, *'to explain a custom whose real origin was forgotten, but whose performance would secure tenants' lands under the new regime'*. Now the bailiff represents the Lord of the Manor of Whitby, and only one family takes part.

At 9am on the eve of Ascension Day they drive stakes with an ancient mallet into the foreshore below the high tide mark near Boyes Staithe in Whitby harbour. They then weave osiers among them to form a 'hedge' strong enough to withstand three tides. This done, the bailiff of the Court Leet of Fyling blows the horn and shouts '*out upon ye, out upon ye*'. The penance 'hedge' is a token, but if they fail to make it, or the hedge is swept away by the tides, the tenancy will be lost, so the story goes ...

PIERS

Extending a practical function (to act as landing stages for steam ships full of holidaymakers), the first 'pleasure pier' was built on the Isle of Wight, at Ryde in 1814, as the gentry began to flock to the fashionable new resorts. From Clevedon pier in Somerset the occasional pleasure cruise can still be taken, but at its peak in the early 1900s it served four different steamer companies and, as late as 1939, was playing host to at least twenty ships a week. The same was true of the other piers – nearly sixty in total – dotted along the English coast. Their elegance and variety speaks of cast iron and concrete, colour and restraint, tranquillity and boisterousness.

Clevedon, Somerset.

Factory shut-downs, bank holidays, an extended railway network and the first glimmerings of disposable income opened up the coast to workers and city dwellers. Where city fathers saw opportunity to attract them, piers were built. The National Piers Society's figures show that in the 1860s and 1870s, on average, two piers were opening every year.

People were beginning to enjoy piers in their own right. A dramatic walk out over the waves, as John Betjeman put it, '*to walk on the sea without the disadvantage of being sick*'; a new perspective of the resort and coastline; the healthy sea air – all came together to increase piers' appeal. When the steamers' popularity waned and there was no longer any need for a landing station, the pier became an amusement arcade or a cafeteria, a ballroom or a theatre, or somewhere simply to fish or look longingly out to sea.

Decay began in the 1930s. The inter-war years were no time for holidays or for the already struggling steamers. Storm, flame and accident often proved fatal during these austerities. Many piers were breached to prevent their use by invaders. To survive, many 'moved with the times' and became gaudy money pits. Others suffered the ignominy of slow erosion.

The West Pier at Brighton, designed by pier engineer *par excellence* Eugenius Birch and opened in 1866, was closed in 1975. After a quarter of a century of decline, with discussions well advanced for its restoration

Cleethorpes, Lincolnshire.

and redevelopment, it was almost destroyed in two suspicious fires in 2003. Then, in 2004, it suffered storm damage sufficient to cause English Heritage to withdraw support. This is a multiple tragedy, as the pier was much favoured by starlings, who, dispossessed after the hurricanes of 1987, had taken to roosting there. Fifty thousand wheeling birds may be lost to the evening sky and will no doubt be persecuted wherever they try to gather.

But the end-of-the-pier show has not happened. Since the 1960s popular interest has grown, some communities banding together to recover their piers. Clevedon – *'the most beautiful in England'*, in Betjeman's opinion – collapsed while being load-tested for insurance in 1970, and lay neglected. The district council applied to demolish it in 1979, but was defeated at a public inquiry. The enthusiasm, hard work and fundraising efforts of the Clevedon Pier Preservation Trust saw that it was re-opened within ten years of the application, and by 1995 it had already been visited by half a million people. Southwold pier in Suffolk opened in 2001, the first pier built since the 1950s.

PILLBOXES

Skulking in bushes beside rivers or brazenly lounging on the beach, pillboxes are a reminder of the peril felt during 1940 that invasion might come from the sea and up the valleys, as indeed had happened during the so-called Dark Ages.

Many were simple circular or pentagonal flat-topped structures made from reinforced concrete (fifteen inches or more thick), reminiscent of the faceted boxes used by pharmacists to dispense pills in the early twentieth century. The horizontal slits for guns enabled a 360-degree field of fire. Perhaps six thousand of the original 28,000 survive in Britain, a few from the First World War. The most intact line of 280 pillboxes and machine-gun nests can be found from Seaton in south Devon to

Bridgwater in north Somerset. Pillboxes followed railways and canals, as well as roads and rivers. To the roof of the Art Deco Bishopstone Station in Sussex a double-layer octagonal pillbox was added.

In Northumberland, between Cresswell and Widdrington, Druridge Bay is watched over by a ruined bothie; it was built to disguise its function as defensive emplacement. At Alnmouth a stone building of uncertain origin, locally held to be a guano import shed from the nineteenth century, was refashioned with twenty gun slits by 1940. On the Yorkshire coast some pillboxes have ears, with room for a machine gun, on each side; at Fraisthorpe near Bridlington one is now stranded on the beach.

A small cylinder of concrete with slits at Kimmeridge Bay, Dorset bears the ridges of its corrugated-iron mould. Tilting precariously, it awaits its fate at the hands of the sea. Heavily undermined by the water, one of a group of low pillboxes clad in beach cobbles at Porlock Bay, Somerset is wonderfully disguised. Wavy edges to the concrete roof, a Devonian idiosyncrasy, are visible at Torcross. Some of these memorials to Churchill's promise that *'we shall fight on the beaches'* are now being listed as ancient monuments. On Burgh Island, Devon a restored pillbox was on sale for £70,000 in 2004, advertised with a view to die for.

Kimmeridge beach, Dorset.

PORTLAND LERRETS

The lerret is a 'double ender', said to get its name from the first of its kind, *Lady of Loretto*. Its unique home is Chesil Bank in Dorset; its shape, similar to that of Norse longships, enabled it to land on the steep, shifting shingle and launch into often ferocious seas. Up to seventeen feet long and six feet wide, lerrets were used for mackerel fishing with seine nets; latterly with six oars, now with four, strong arms rowed them through the surf. Landing was just as tricky as launching and was done swiftly by a beach crew to prevent the boat being overwhelmed by the waves. Once ashore, the boat was hauled up the beach over the oars. Its shape was adopted for most ships' lifeboats, as Eric McKee wrote, adding: '*What appears to be a simple canoe form is a successful compromise between buoyancy and power.*'

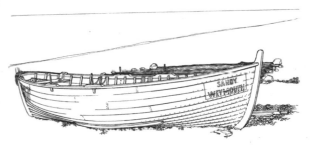

PUNCH AND JUDY

Every May a surfeit of Punches and Judys gathers at London's Covent Garden. They celebrate Samuel Pepys, who wrote in 1662 about seeing Punchinello from Italy. Puppets were already popular in Tudor England, associated with the fair, but these characters have outlasted them all as

popular open-air entertainment. With the railways and rising interest in taking the sea air, the puppet booth found a new habitat and took on the stripes of the seaside.

The plot atrophied in the 1820s after being written down by a journalist, yet every show has its own script and the making of the 'swazzle' is personal – this metal mouth-part changes the voice to the characteristic high, vibrating tone of Mr Punch. Somehow the Punch and Judy show embodies the wild aspects of popular culture, shifting, offensive, anarchic.

QUICKSAND

Stories of old grey mares being sucked under the quicksand and of people being overtaken by tides roaring in 'swifter than a galloping horse' should put anyone off crossing the vast sand expanses of Morecambe Bay or the Solway Firth, where safe ways across the sand are called waths.

In Lancashire, North of the Sands, the milestone at Cartmel offers the siren call '*Lancaster over sands 15 miles/ Ulverston over sands 7 miles*', saving ten and four miles respectively. Before the building of the railway in 1857 from Hest Bank to Kents Bank, many did not make it across this treacherous terrain, where the Kent and Keer disgorge their water through shifting patterns of silt. The river Keer has dangerous 'poos', or rivulets, with quicksand on the inside of meanders, and the channels are always on the move. Deep freshwater springs also bring problems.

Travellers were tempted by the short cuts, but only fools would go without a guide. Indeed so important was the task that in the sixteenth century King John made it a royal appointment. The current Queen's Guide to the Sands of Morecambe Bay, Cedric Robinson, tests the cross-sands walk in his bare feet to really feel the texture and micro-movement of the sand. Only then will he lead walkers in summer across the eight to twelve miles to Grange-over-Sands. When people get into trouble, the Arnside fire engine may come to the rescue, and Bay Hovercraft Rescue has built two amphibious vehicles, now on constant standby.

RIAS

The coastline of the South has some spectacular indentations. Examples include Pagham and Chichester harbours in Sussex; Portsmouth harbour and Southampton Water in Hampshire, etched into the low-lying coastal plain; and in Devon and Cornwall complex creek systems embedded in steep valleys. Since the Ice Age southern England has been tilting into the sea, which has also been rising and has invaded low-lying land. The drowned valleys, or rias, provide welcome havens, making these places the best for watching birds and boats in the South.

They form a particular and beautiful feature of the South West. For those on land the rias create long diversions, but ferries and a high population of boats reduce isolation. In Devon and Cornwall the water is deep and excellent for shipping and sailing. The cross-profiles of the valleys are steeply plunging, and woodland that frequently comes down to the water's edge makes the smaller rias intimate and sheltered. In the

South Hams of Devon the Erme is barely serpentine, but narrow and secluded; the high tide kisses the trees. The Dart is long and winding, and the Kingsbridge estuary has a handful of side creeks. Villages cling to the steep slopes, as at Noss Mayo on the Yealm, which is full of moored yachts and fishing boats. Remote creeks and scattered marshes attract otters, wildfowl and waders, including the golden plover and black-tailed godwit.

Plymouth and Saltash share the giant estuary of the Tamar and Tavy, providing an important harbour for naval vessels. In Cornwall the Fowey estuary runs straight to the north between steep slopes, offering a deep harbour capable of taking ships loading one and a half million tons of china clay. The Fal estuary is very broad across the Carrick Roads; Falmouth is an industrial port, the docks vying with marinas. This is the largest, most westerly sheltered haven on the south coast.

River Yealm, Noss Mayo, Devon.

SALT MARSHES

On coastal salt marshes pioneering, salt-loving plants gain a foothold on the land just above inter-tidal mud-flats. These marshes, regularly washed by the tide, are among the most dynamic habitats on the planet. They form only in a few sheltered places, in estuaries, saline lagoons, behind barrier islands and on beach plains. At the cutting edge, nearest the sea, grows the brave glasswort salicornia, or marsh samphire (sometimes sold as 'sandfire'), that withstands soaking by six hundred tides a year. On the quieter, landward edge grow plants able to cope with only occasional inundation: sea and salt marsh rushes, golden samphire, shrubby sea blite and sea wormwood. In the middle reaches of the marsh, sea purslane, sea lavender, sea plantain, thrift and greater sea spurrey and salt marsh grass find a home.

Most of our eighty thousand acres of salt marsh are concentrated in four areas: the Thames estuary, the Essex coast, Liverpool and Morecambe Bay and the Wash. Each has a characteristic flora, on fine sediments on the east coast, on a sandy base on the west.

Salt marshes are famously productive. The annual growth of salt marsh grass and cord grass rivals the output of a tropical rainforest – up to eighty ounces of green vegetation per square yard in a year. Much of this organic wealth flows back into the estuary to support fish and invertebrates, including oysters, mussels and cockles, which thrive in the calm, nutrient-rich waters and are in turn eaten by birds.

In Essex the Blackwater estuary supports up to sixteen thousand wildfowl and thirty thousand waders. Redshank may even nest on the marsh, their eggs surviving the odd brush with the tide. The salt marshes of the Solway Firth in Cumberland regularly host more than 120,000 wintering wildfowl and are internationally important for wintering geese, including the entire breeding population of the Spitzbergen barnacle goose. Along this coast sheep and cattle are grazed on rich common marshes regulated by a committee, which works out the stints (numbers of animals shared out according to the carrying capacity of the land), and watched over by marsh wardens.

These areas hide reminders of our past activities, sparring or working with the sea, for example winning salt, as at Salt Cotes and Crosscanonby in Cumberland. Now scale is the problem – large coastal developments, such as the Felixstowe dock extension in Suffolk and the Thames Gateway development, threaten and destroy these unique places. Agriculture takes its toll, too: in the Wash around two thousand acres of salt marsh were converted to farming between 1970 and 1980. The sinking of south-east England – by about two millimetres a year – and rising sea levels linked to global warming are squeezing salt marshes against sea walls, which prevent their migration inland. As the marsh disappears, the waves begin to erode the sea walls themselves. 'Managed realignment' – including allowing the sea to flow onto land behind existing sea walls – offers a better prospect for the future. In 2002 controlled breaches were made in the sea wall at Abbotts Hall, a historic coastal farm eight miles south of Colchester, as the first step in re-creating protective salt marshes along the Essex coast.

SAND-DUNES

Paradise for children and lovers (although not at the same time), sand-dunes are miniature, soft mountain ranges by the sea. England boasts nearly thirty thousand acres of sand-dunes, concentrated on the coasts of Northumberland, Lincolnshire, Norfolk, Kent, Dorset, Devon, Cornwall, Lancashire, Westmorland and Cumberland. Behind the beach, accumulations of wind-blown sand develop into low hills of bare, shifting sand, joined by semi-stable larger dunes, sometimes rising up to one hundred feet and held by tenacious marram grass. It may be joined by sea holly, sea spurges and scores of other distinctive flowering plants, as well as mosses and lichens. Terns, shelducks, oystercatchers and more find

Formby Dunes, Lancashire.

The distribution of coastal sand-dunes.

nesting places among the dunes, as do sand wasps and mining bees. The Lancashire dunes at Ainsdale famously play host to some two thousand natterjack toads.

These magnificent coastal landscapes are highly mobile, precariously balanced between the erosion and deposition of sand, and need to be able to migrate inland. The construction of sea defences or the stabilisation of dunes for golf-courses, housing developments and holiday resorts can seriously disrupt movement; more than half of the 121 dune sites are now eroding away as a result.

SEA CAVES

Once you have seen wave upon wave bearing down on the Atlantic coast of Cornwall, it becomes obvious that any slight weakness in the hardest of rock faces will be excavated without mercy. The sea cave is one result. Kynance Cove on the Lizard peninsula, with its white sand and colourful beached-whale rocks, hides caves in the polished serpentine rock, exciting despite their prosaic names – the Kitchen, the Parlour and the Ladies' Bathing Pool. Tennyson ruminated in one of the caves here, '*watching wave rainbows*'. We may catch a glimpse once again of the chough, that shining black bird with the handsome red beak, which makes its nest in caves and rock fissures.

Dark caves, light caves, dripping, dropping – despite their clear dangers we are drawn to explore them. Enticing and alarming us with associations of past and present smuggling and ancient tales, the presence of a cave on the headland or at the back of the beach makes a difference, intensifies the experience, often makes a sacred place. Merlin's Cave at Tintagel in Cornwall offers both natural grandeur and all the mystery of Arthurian legend. Walking into darkness and then discovering that the cave is cut right through to meet the sea on the other side heightens the power of the place.

Lundy, the Scillies and the Farne Islands have caves of note, while whole coastal counties have few or none, such as Cumberland, Lancashire, Cheshire and the east coast, from Essex up to north Yorkshire. Where there are awesome cliffs many caves are visible only from the sea. Secret and often unapproachable they remain one of the few parts of these islands fairly untouched by human activity, a boon to the sea birds and seals. The fretted cliffs around Flamborough Head, Yorkshire offer tall clefts, or geos, and chalk caves of all kinds, only viewable from boats leaving North Landing. Robin Lyth Cave is named after a fictitious smuggler from R. D. Blackmore's *Mary Anerley*. Big caves are explorable in Thornwick Bay at low tide. Blackhall Rocks in County Durham is famous for its dramatic sea caves and stacks in the soft magnesian limestone.

The Chelsea Speleological Society made an important discovery while surveying Canterbury Cave in St Margaret's Bay, Kent in 1975. Assuming it to have been etched by the sea, despite its name not appearing on maps before 1960, they found an extensive network of caves in the chalk. Mostly above the high-water mark, it proved to be a relict system formed by an underground stream, revealed when the sea cut back the face of the cliff.

Beachy Head Cave in Sussex is the longest in chalk; so far explored are 1,160 feet of passages, some inhabited by spiders, flies and moths. Although changed by rockfalls, the main cave entrance lies fourteen feet above the high-water mark; again, this must have been worn by a stream flowing above a flint layer.

For a perfect line of little caves from which to understand the processes, a visit to Durdle Cove in Dorset will reveal a honeycomb line just above the high-water mark, picking out weakness where rock has sheared against rock.

SEA FISH

The North Sea has increased in temperature by one degree Celsius in just 25 years. Eighteen species of fish, including haddock and cod, have moved northwards, some by more than seventy miles; others have sought deeper waters. Changing seas driven by climatic shifts have also brought tuna, new kinds of shark and sea-horses to our coasts. Occasional subtropical fish are turning up in nets, and sardines, anchovies, John Dory and red mullet are becoming more common.

Our staple sea fish have been suffering decline after a century of overfishing. Salmon are scarce, and the once-ubiquitous cod and skate are on the way to becoming rare delicacies. This, coupled with international legislation – and the availability of easier work in other trades – has turned an industry that provided the main employment in many coastal towns into a white dwarf.

The fishermen's intimate knowledge and the fish that were their livelihood are beginning to slip from the everyday. For a lifetime the harbours of East Anglia and the North East were driven by herrings; Yarmouth, Norfolk was where, until as late as the 1960s, Scots and

Northumbrian girls known as 'herring lasses' would travel each year to work on fish processing. Yarmouth still has herrings on its coat of arms; the town was famous for its smoked, or 'bloated', herrings – bloaters. Now herrings are imported from Norway, having been fished out from around the east coast of England.

The fish of the North Sea were plentiful. Berwick-upon-Tweed in Northumberland still crowns a Salmon Queen each July. In the North East there were mackerel between July and October, salmon and trout from March to September and haddock from November, as well as turbot (locally called brat), whiting, sole (dab), plaice on Dogger Bank, cod, lamprey (soocker) and skate (ginny). Fish were the lifeblood of Seahouses, Boulmer and North Shields in Northumberland and South Shields in County Durham. Now the fish quay at North Shields is better known for an annual music festival.

In Yorkshire Hull and the Humber were alive with fishing boats until the end of the 1970s; the city now boasts a visitor centre called The Deep. Across the estuary in Lincolnshire, Grimsby, with its football club The Mariners, was once 'Home of the Haddock'. Now it is the home of the National Fishing Heritage Centre, but still one of the country's top fish markets.

Dover sole had some geographical allegiance; to the fishermen around Kent and Sussex soles were slips, dogfish were bone dogs or bull-huss, flounders were eyeballers. Sea bass can still be found in the Essex estuaries of the Colne and Blackwater, but warmer seas are spreading their range. The Channel and the Solent held skate, mackerel, whiting, cod, plaice and pilchard. Occasionally Royal Sturgeon would appear at Mudeford and Christchurch in Hampshire, but Poole in Dorset and Beer and Sidmouth in Devon were the main centres of industry on the south coast. Plymouth Sound in Devon has the country's only Steven's goby. Weymouth, Dorset was famed for red mullet (which is now being found in the Thames estuary and beyond). The seaside rock pools of Devon, Dorset and Cornwall still have their shannies and blennies.

On the flat Somerset coast around the mouth of the Parrett the last of the mud-horse fishermen are still working. James Crowden explained: '*their method of fishing has changed little since neolithic times. Nets strung out on poles ... The mud-horse is a sledge with a curved front which is pushed out [across the mud] and then brought back to help carry the catch.*' Haaf nets still cross the bays around Silloth and Maryport in Cumberland, as they have since the Danes arrived eleven hundred years ago. Liverpool and Fleetwood, Lancashire were the heart of the Irish Sea fishing business. Morecambe Bay, with its ferocious tides, is where whitefish and flatfish are found, the latter known as 'flukes' in Flookburgh, Lancashire, perhaps the origin of the place-name.

Pilchards made the familiar stereotype of the 'Cornish fishing village' and filled many a Stargazy pie. Huer's houses were built as lookout towers to scan for the shoals; one survives near Newquay. Fresh fish is still landed and traded across Cornwall, but, although Newlyn and Padstow stand out, like Brixham in Devon, with thriving fish markets, the future is uncertain.

SEA FORTS

For centuries England guarded against sea attack with land-based defences. In the mid-1800s Lord Palmerston went one step further, placing forts on islands in estuaries to attack invading navies before they got within range of land. In the Medway estuary in Kent artist Stephen Turner worked on Hoo Island in 1998. To him, Darnet and Hoo forts '*stand like Scylla and Charybdis down river from the former Royal Navy Dockyard at Chatham. They exist today as wonderful overgrown and derelict follies, home to all manner of wildlife.*'

Bull Sand fort was built in 1915 on a sandbank near Spurn Head, Yorkshire to protect the Humber, together with Haile Sand fort, a mile off the coast, which is visible from the sea front at Humberston,

Lincolnshire. Both are armour-plated over concrete and look grim yet vulnerable, like floating islands.

Sailing out of Portsmouth harbour in Hampshire, Spit Bank, Horse Sands and No Man's Land forts erupt out of the Solent like forbidding props from a James Bond film. The mechanisation of warfare in the twentieth century pressed existing forts into new action as gun emplacements, magazines and bases. A few new ones appeared.

Off Whitstable in Kent, Redsand fort's extraordinary array of seven towers (now without linking walkways), each raised high above the sea on stilts, looks rather like a gathering of box cameras on legs. Guy Maunsell designed similar sea forts for the Mersey, the Humber and the Thames during the Second World War. After being abandoned in 1956 their ambiguous legal status proved ideal for the unlicensed pirate radio stations of the 1960s. Screaming Lord Sutch, for example, used Shivering Sands, seven miles off Herne Bay in Kent, as the base for Sutch Radio, later Radio City. Roughs Tower, off Essex, had perhaps the most unusual change of fortunes. Paddy Roy Bates and his family moved there in 1967 and continue in residence, having successfully claimed sovereignty. They are now the royal family of the Principality of Sealand.

Fort Brockhurst, Gosport, Hampshire (a Palmerston fort).

SEA-MARKS

The singular chapel on St Aldhelm's Head, just 35 feet square, may have been used by mariners since the twelfth century as a landmark or sea-mark to guide them around the dangerous cliffs and rocks of the Isle of Purbeck, Dorset. Around the coast, church steeples were often used as navigational aids, some perhaps having beacon fires on the towers.

Day marks were erected to aid daylight approach to harbours if conspicuous rocks, natural features or buildings could not be used. Turner's Cornish painting *The Entrance to Fowey Harbour*, with its tempestuous sea and sky, gives ample reason for the presence of Gribbin Beacon; the red and white tower, more than eighty feet high, on Gribbin Head is prominent from every sea direction and denotes the otherwise cryptic way to shelter in the Fowey estuary.

Rodney Legg described lining up to enter Portland Harbour in Dorset, where '*two slender concrete faced pyramids, twenty feet high … stand on the grassy slopes above West Bottom at about 510 feet and 540 feet above sea level. They are set as sea-marks, which, when lined up, show the safe approach from the south. The passage they pinpoint is from south-by-south-west to north-by-north-east, charting a course between the perilous ledges off Portland Bill and the parlous offshore Shambles sandbank.*'

Vessels would pick up a red light from the 54-foot-high east light if they were approaching on an unsafe bearing towards Whitby harbour in Yorkshire; now a red light for the same purpose shines out from the steep steps up to St Mary's Church.

SEA TRACTOR

If you want to catch the South Sands Ferry at Salcombe in Devon, '*a unique motorised landing stage*' will drive you precariously but high above the water to the boat.

But at Burgh Island, further west in Devon, an unmatched creature thrills children and grizzled skippers when the tide is in. Sea Tractor III,

commissioned by the island's owners as an all-tide conveyance, sporting the Royal Ensign, stands quiet by the Pilchard Inn at the end of the sands that link the island with Bigbury-on-Sea. When the tide is out one can walk across the isthmus to appreciate island life for a few hours. But when the tide is in, the Sea Tractor crawls carefully across the sand, diversifying its quarter-mile route to deliver its slightly scared passengers back and forth.

It is like a piece of the Forth Bridge gone feral: heavy tubes form the chassis, a high platform six feet up is contained by wooden planking, and open, but roofed, seating rolls on big, soft tyres.

SHELLFISH

Our inshore waters have provided some our most fascinating food: Morecambe Bay shrimps, Stiffkey cockles, Cromer crabs, Whitstable oysters, Brancaster mussels.

From Norfolk, Stiffkey blues range from '*pale lavender to a dark grey-blue*', according to Laura Mason and Catherine Brown. At one time they were called bluestones, the colour coming from the local mud and sand, where they live a few inches below the surface in large congregations. In the 1880s the cockles were collected at low tide by local women, using short-handled, broad rakes and nets. They were steamed and used in soups and pies and sold at seaside stalls, eaten (boiled) with vinegar and pepper. In addition to these places around the Wash, the other main shellfish-gathering area is the Thames estuary.

They are still a favourite food along the Thames and Essex coast. Carol Donaldson writes: '*While many East End traditions have died away, the displaced Cockneys of Havering [Essex] are still busy winkle picking and whelk swallowing and this peculiarity is not just the preserve of the old. Young, shaven-headed lads are dousing their cockles in vinegar at a weekend and ordering jellied eels by the pint. Maybe it's our proximity to the Thames and its seafood centres of Leigh-on-Sea and Southend that gives us a love of these unappetising creatures. The ex-Cockneys keep business brisk among the cockle sheds lining the front at Leigh, which trades in five thousand tonnes of cockles a year.*'

Despite this local trade, many lost their appetite when some cockle beds were closed due to contamination by algal toxins. Morecambe Bay in Lancashire has gained notoriety for the exploitation of collectors and shellfish, following the drownings of foreign workers unused to the ferocious tides. In 2005 the Morecambe Bay cockle beds were closed to allow the diminishing stocks to recover. On the Solway Firth, Cumberland and other estuaries conservationists are worried that suction dredging has replaced raking, depleting not only the cockles but a whole host of marine invertebrates, and disturbing and removing the food of wading birds such as oystercatchers, which are adept at opening the hard cockle shells, and herring gulls. The latter, finding the shells difficult to prise apart, have resorted to taking them to shore and dropping them from a fair height onto a hard surface. Today most cockles are sent to Spain, France and Holland.

Mussels anchor themselves to rocks and piers. Most mussel fisheries are on the east, south and west coasts. They have been farmed at

Brancaster Staithe in north Norfolk for more than a century. One-year-old mussels are collected and moved to the lays – beds – in tidal creeks, where they are left to grow for a couple of years before harvesting. Brancaster fishermen used to collect whelks as well, but all that remains are the whelk sheds, where now mussels and oysters are purified. These days whelks – marine snails – once so popular with Londoners, find their main market in South Korea. They are collected from baited buckets dropped into the sea off places such as Beer in Devon, and transported to Fleetwood in Lancashire, where they are pressure cooked, processed and frozen for air freighting.

Norfolk's Cromer crabs thrive in the chalk reefs that run out from the coast, producing the country's sweetest crustaceans. About a dozen boats look after around two hundred crab pots. Edible crabs are caught in many places, such as Start Point near Salcombe in Devon, Scarborough in Yorkshire and the Solway Firth, where they appear on the menus of local restaurants. Lobster pots are piled high on beaches and quays from Hastings, Sussex to St Ives, Cornwall. Willow lobster pots are still made, although largely they have been replaced by plastic and steel.

Morecambe Bay, Lancashire.

Shrimps have been netted at Morecambe Bay since the late 1700s, caught in shallow waters from nobbies, or from the shore using horses or tractors and long nets. They are cooked in Flookburgh within half an hour of being landed. In 2000 thirteen million pots of Bob Baxter's Morecambe Bay shrimps were sold by mail order.

SHINGLE

Almost a third of the English coastline is shingle, coated in coarse pebbles, often flint eroded from chalk cliffs or carried to the beach by rivers and glaciers. Sound clues alone identify these beaches – the word shingle is thought to derive from the strange, shimmering clinking of the pebbles as they are raked by the waves. Hastings, Brighton and Worthing in Sussex are fine examples, thronging with swimmers and sunbathers in summer. At Chesil in Dorset the fishermen landing on the shingle bank

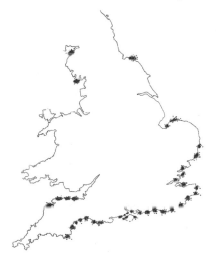

The distribution of coastal shingle.

at night or in fog can judge their position by the size of the pebbles. Up the road the prehistoric inhabitants of Maiden Castle amassed vast hordes of sling stones taken from the beach.

Shingle is notoriously challenging to walk along. Fishermen and their families living on Dungeness in Kent wore wooden flip-flops called baxters or backstays over their shoes, which worked like a kind of snow-shoe.

The bleak, wind-swept spit of shingle at Orford Ness in Suffolk is our largest vegetated shingled spit; it houses a now-derelict military base, where radar was invented.

The largest shingle beach by far is the great triangle of Dungeness, covering nearly four thousand acres and formed where the Channel and North Sea waters meet. At places the shingle is more than fifty feet thick, formed into ridges and hollows by the waves. During the twentieth century this unique place has been much damaged by military training, the construction of a nuclear power station and shingle extraction – half of Dungeness now lies under railways and motorways elsewhere. The spit supports an astonishing array of plants, ranging from yellow-horned poppy and sea pea, sea campion and shepherd's cress, to hollies, mosses and lichens that have lived on the beach for hundreds of years.

SHIPPING FORECAST

'There are warnings of gales in Sole; Lundy; Fastnet …' The litany of the area forecasts for shipping lulls listeners to BBC Radio 4 just after midnight and wakes them at 05.36 GMT, a daily reminder of our island state. But, warm and snug, it is hard to muster the idea that those same reassuring tones convey harsh realities aboard ship or smack out there in Rockall, Dogger or Trafalgar.

The more intimate waters to twelve miles off coast have their own shorthand listings immediately after the Shipping Forecast, each area enunciated before a brief run-down of conditions to be met heading out

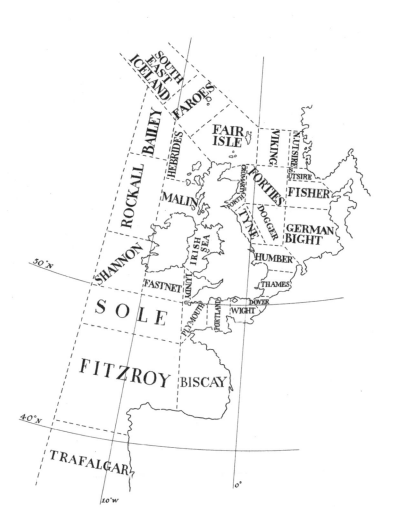

SOUTH EAST ICELAND

FAROES

FAIR ISLE

VIKING

N.UTSIRE

S.UTSIRE

BAILEY

HEBRIDES

FORTIES

FISHER

ROCKALL

MALIN

CROMARTY

FORTH

TYNE

DOGGER

GERMAN BIGHT

SHANNON

IRISH SEA

HUMBER

FASTNET

LUNDY

THAMES

SOLE

PLYMOUTH

PORTLAND

DOVER

WIGHT

FITZROY

BISCAY

TRAFALGAR

50°N

40°N

10°W

0°

Shipping forecast areas.

or home. From the Wash to North Foreland, for example: '*north becoming variable or northeast 3 or 4; fair; moderate or good*'. Twenty-four hours of wind, weather, visibility and sea state are each followed by the next day's outlook, and a general three-day outlook concludes the broadcast.

Authentic found poems every one.

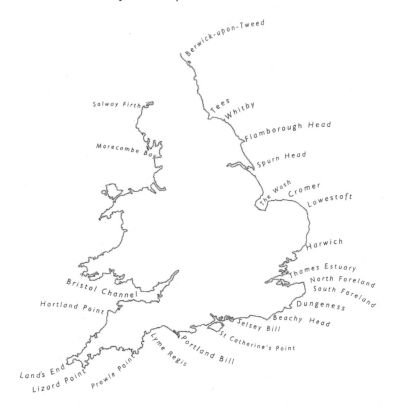

Inshore waters areas.

SOUND MIRRORS

Known in Kent as 'listening ears', these huge concrete acoustic discs can be found on the coasts of Kent, County Durham and Yorkshire. Sound amplifiers were developed from 1914 by a Professor Mather, to locate and give early warning of enemy aircraft. His first experiment was a sixteen-foot-diameter disc cut out of a chalk cliff at Binbury Manor Farm, between Sittingbourne and Maidstone, Kent; he claimed he could detect a Zeppelin twenty miles away.

During the First World War sound mirrors were being constructed along the east coast. A large, freestanding structure with a fifteen-foot-diameter concrete dish (looking rather like an open mouth) was built at Kilnsea, Spurn Head in Yorkshire; others were positioned at Hartlepool and Redcar on either side of the Tees estuary, and at Boulby, Yorkshire, on top of the cliff, facing out to sea. The plaque on the sound mirror at Redcar reads: '*The sound of approaching aircraft was reflected off the concave "mirror" surface and received into a trumpet mounted on a steel column. The trumpet was connected to a stethoscope used by the operator or "listener", and the part of the dish that produced the most sound indicated the direction of the approaching aircraft.*'

Research continued between the wars and by 1923 a twenty-foot-diameter sound mirror, with new electric microphones and an improved receiving trumpet, had been built into a bank backed by a solid slab of concrete at The Roughs in Hythe, Kent, able to detect aircraft twelve miles away. Dr W. S. Tucker, appointed Director of Acoustical Research in 1925, planned to build '*a chain of twenty-foot sound mirrors along the south coast*'. Two were built in 1928, one perched on top of Abbot's Cliff at Lydden Spout in Dover, Kent, which now looks like a modern sculpture – a concrete bowl cut out of a square, flat surface, supported by triangular slabs at either side – and the other at Great Stone, Denge, on the Dungeness peninsula in Kent. This was the first of three sound mirrors at

Denge, which have been scheduled by English Heritage because they '*form a unique collection*' showing a progression of designs. They have been made unstable by gravel extraction, but are now being repaired and underpinned.

By 1939, due to the development of radar, the Acoustical Research Station had been closed down and the sound mirrors abandoned. Some have been lost to coastal erosion or demolished. But the remaining structures have inspired Danish artist Lise Autogena to create her own benign Channel Communication Amplifiers. Placed at Folkestone, Kent and Sangatte, France, they will, according to the Arts Council, '*be perfectly aligned to receive and transmit not only the sounds of the sea, but also the human voice across 45 kilometres of water*'.

STACKS

They may be echoes of beautiful arches or treacherous cracks, but detachment is the aspiration of sea stacks, to become rock pillars uniquely sculpted by the sea.

The Needles have become icons well beyond the Isle of Wight, Hampshire; they tell a story of chalk, crumpling and constant harrying. We know them as molar-like rocks, but charts of the early seventeenth century show a group of pencils to the north and Lot's Wife, or Cleopatra's Needle, in between – this was the last to fall in 1764. Frenchman's Cellar, Old Pepper, Roe Hall and Wedge survive as dangerous sentinels, pointing across the bay to Old Harry ('*his Satanic majesty*') and his crumbling Wife, who sacrifice themselves for the Isle of Purbeck. This great headland seems to spawn stacks. In aerial view or from the sea it looks as if great bites have been taken out of the chalk; you sense a production line of tough little promontories bravely standing up, better than the miniature coves, to the gnawing of the waves.

From Flamborough Head to Bempton in Yorkshire bays carved between high chalk headlands have bookends, such as Adam and Eve pinnacles and the King and Queen. The Parson and Clerk are fashioned from the brown-red sandstone of Dawlish in Devon; they trudge like pilgrims, their robes heavy with the sea, although their story is one of blasphemy and dining with the devil.

Like all and sundry gathering for a parish moot, the varied stacks at Bedruthan Steps in Cornwall stand with their feet in the sand, disturbing

Purbeck, Dorset.

the progress of the tide. Bedruthan was a Celtic giant, who found these stepping-stones useful. One of the rocks recalled for some the profile of Queen Bess; another, Samaritan Rock, reminds of a ship wrecked in the 1840s, allowing serious beach-combing to supplement a poor living.

We marvel at their endurance, their shapes and forms, the refuge they give to seabirds, but stacks are anthropomorphised and satanised for good reason. These recognisable rocks have always given seamen and fishermen a way of knowing where they are; the stories attached to them help to embed the shape, position and danger in the mind.

STARFISH

Starfish come in many forms, from the commonest five-pointed kind to bright red, twelve-legged varieties that look more like sunbursts. Fishermen despise them for their light-fingered prowess in decimating shellfish. They have a lot of names for them: in 1970 Willy Elmer gathered words for starfish from fishermen all around the coast, as part of his doctorate on English Dialect – the Terminology of Fishing.

Sand star.

Common starfish.

Cushion star.

Common sunstar.

SURFING

On boards made by local coffin makers, the early surfers were inspired by stories from their Anzac and South African comrades during the First World War.

The best surfing beaches in Cornwall rely on great swells to hit the coast from the low pressure weather systems in the Atlantic; the best come in the autumn and winter months. Perranporth is said to have seen the first surfing in Britain. Fistral Bay is the best beach for surf, and the possibility of the local council selling part of it provoked worries about restricted access. Watergate Bay lures beginners and those who wish to experiment with kite surfing.

Newquay attracts a hundred thousand people to the World Rip Curl Boardmasters Festival. The Cribber, a legendary thirty-foot wave named after the reef half a mile off Newquay at the north end of Towan Head, has attracted attention since 1966, when it was ridden by three visiting Australian surfers, rarely achieved since. Artificial surfing reefs are mooted off Tolcarne at Newquay and Bournemouth, Hampshire.

There are long-established surfing beaches in Devon and off Cayton Bay, near Scarborough, Yorkshire. Newcastle has Long Sands, north of Tynemouth, and the mouth of the river between the harbour piers, where the Black Middens rocks create a reef break.

All beaches, though, have their points of interest, known intimately by regulars: the best part of the tide, local weather, dangerous rips and rocks below the surface. Surfers Against Sewage, based in Cornwall, campaigns imaginatively for clean seas for all of us.

THAMES SAILING BARGES

Following a pattern used by the Dutch in the Middle Ages, flat-bottomed barges were worked from the seventeenth to the twentieth centuries along the shallow creeks and rivers of the 'barge coast' of Suffolk, Essex and north Kent. The Kent brick-makers Eastwoods built up a fleet of seventy barges – 'brickies' – with their own livery in the last half of the nineteenth century. Spurred by competition from steam trains, Henry Dodd started the annual Sailing Barge Matches in 1863; this inspired refinements, resulting in faster boats that proved a match for the railways.

The versatility of the Thames sailing barge was extraordinary. Its flat bottom allowed it to go far upstream and settle steadily on the mud as the tide dropped. Its masts and complex rigging could be dramatically dropped for 'shooting' the bridges, and rapidly re-erected by a crew of just two plus a 'huffler' (an extra hand). Into London they might carry bricks and cement from Milton Creek in Kent, or hay and root crops from Suffolk, returning with horse manure for the fields. They could even sail empty, despite their lack of a keel, since a leeboard could be lowered when sailing to windward.

The showy red-brown sails of the Thames barge were dressed with fish oils, horse urine and red ochre to lengthen their lives. The flamboyance of a large sprit sail, foresail, topsail, mizzen and bowsprit jib standing above a wide, twenty-by-eighty-foot wooden hull still turns heads along their homeriver and neighbouring Medway and Blackwater estuaries. Numbers have dropped from eight thousand to just thirty since 1900, but they remain much loved and respected as the biggest boat to be sailed by just two people before the advent of new technology. They gather for racing from Solent to Swale to Colne throughout the summer, and can usually be seen at St Katharine Docks in London, Maldon Quay in Essex (where there is a Sailing Barge Heritage Centre) and at Standard Quay in Faversham, Kent.

TIDE MILLS

Of the five thousand or so mills mentioned in the Domesday Book, about nine hundred were built on the coast. The tide mill at Woodbridge quay, recently restored, lies on the river Deben in Suffolk, but most were located in the South, especially Hampshire, west Sussex and on the Tamar and Fal estuaries in Devon and Cornwall.

Eling tide mill at Totton near Southampton, on the edge of the New Forest, is the only surviving tide mill in the world producing flour daily using traditional methods. First built more than nine hundred years ago, it has been rebuilt and renovated many times since, most recently in the eighteenth century. The mill fell into disuse in the 1940s, but was restored over five years to re-open in 1980 as a working mill and museum.

It sits on a causeway, a toll road that links Brokenford to Eling, near the mouth of Bartley Water, which runs into the river Test. At its back the mill-pond contains the tidal water impounded by means of sea hatches with flaps, which are pushed open by the incoming tide and closed as the tide tries to run out. Under control of the miller the water is released through an internal hatch to feed the Poncelet waterwheel (there used to be two), allowing about four hours' milling. At its front was a thriving small harbour, where the mill had its own wharf.

The oldest and largest tide mill in England stands imposingly across the river Lea at Bromley-by-Bow in east London. Built in 1776, it contained three big waterwheels, but they are no longer running. Surviving tide mills are still found at Pomphlett in Devon, Emsworth, Beaulieu as well as Eling in Hampshire, Birdham in west Sussex, Thorrington and Stambridge in Essex and Woodbridge in Suffolk.

TIDES

Twice every day the Thames reveals and then conceals the stairs, beaches and tributaries through the centre of London. The flow of the river is as nothing against the rhythm of the tide, whose mean vertical rise and fall between 21½ and fifteen feet at London Bridge ensures that the tide reaches Teddington, Middlesex, where a weir and lock stop its natural progress. Ships, as well as baby flatfish, take a free ride up-river with the tide; in May young flounder (the size of two fifty-pence pieces) dig into the sand to wait for the next help upstream, just one of 115 fish species that inhabit the tidal Thames.

A bell is rung by the changing tide on the Wandle, a right-bank tributary of the Thames, which takes its name from Wandsworth (not the other way around). The Mersey advances and retreats through Liverpool, the Tyne through Newcastle, and small-town harbours lift and drop their boats onto sand and mud from Polperro, Cornwall to Staithes, Yorkshire. Around England the height of the tide is generally six to sixteen feet, but it can reach 47 feet in the Bristol Channel – one of the highest tidal ranges in the world.

On a quiet day at the coast you can hear the sound change as the tide turns. Tim Baber, musing from his beach hut at Mudeford, Hampshire, embellishes an explanation from *ThreeSixty*, the magazine for surfers: '*The tide is basically the longest wave on earth, responding to planetary forces, with a wavelength of half way around the world. With small local variations, it's a wave that comes twice a day, every day and one that dominates our activities, mood and view.*'

Datum is measured locally from a line on the harbour wall or a mark on the pier; the deviation from this gives the tidal range, and it usually relates to safe passage out of the harbour. In Yarmouth, Isle of Wight, for example, tidal gauges are visible on the pier as you enter and on the 'dolphin' as you leave.

Southampton Water in Hampshire is known for the long hold of high water, resulting from the complications of water running round the Isle of Wight, and these are more accentuated in the harbours at Christ-church, Hampshire and Poole, Dorset, where there are long stands of tide (half-day high tide). In Weymouth harbour the Gulder brings a further echo of this; it is a small flood about 45 minutes after the first low water.

The tide extends to its highest and lowest range at spring tides and varies least at neap tides, each of which occurs twice a month according to the closeness of the moon, which pulls the wandering water a little higher and lower when it is full or new. The highest of the highs and the lowest of the lows occur in March and September around the equinox, again according to the moon, with the help of the sun.

Sea level is rising because of the melting of ice caps and glaciers, a contemporary sign of global warming. But in the south of England the land is also pivoting into the sea as Scotland continues to rebound since shedding its weight of frozen water after the Ice Age. So we shall never see such low tides again, and whenever the chance arises to visit the furthest foreshore we should celebrate Low Tide Days and enjoy archaeological as well as ecological explorations.

The foreshore is a miracle of life chances and life-styles. Different plants and creatures cling to different zones according to their capacity to deal with desiccation, inundation and crashing waves, as well as the local conditions of rock, mud or sand. Acorn barnacles dare no further up the rocks than mean high water of neap tides; sea anemones prefer rock pools; in sand and mud creatures dig in while the tide is out. This littoral zone is where many make their home as part of a life cycle of helpless drifting. It is here, too, that we lose ourselves when the tide is out, focusing on the tiny world of the rock pool, seaweeds, starfish, shells, rippled sand, noisy birds and strange finds.

More than a hundred square miles of sand is exposed in Morecambe Bay, Lancashire at low water. The place's worst reputation is for the rapid return of the tide, which speeds at a jogging pace on its way to high water mark. Working out when it is best to walk over the sands, venture round the point, go beachcombing and leave harbour all require local knowledge and the *Tide Tables*.

For centuries visitors to St Michael's Mount in Cornwall and Lindisfarne in Northumberland have contended with the tides. The causeway to Lindisfarne was part-built in 1954 and completed in 1966, but it is not passable for five hours around each high tide and is still lined by poles for the late or daring pilgrim. When the tide is out a river called the Low is revealed. Before the causeway there were two routes across the sands, lined by poles, and on the three-mile track from Beal shore to Chare Ends there were refuge boxes for those caught short by the sea.

When King Canute, sitting on his throne on the beach, commanded that the tide should not come, he intended to demonstrate to others his limitations, his lack of omnipotence. Although popularly remembered differently, the tale offers wisdom still.

UNLUCKY WORDS

The Isle of Portland has the feel of an ancient and introspective place, but it shares a strange secret. The word ra**it is never used by indigenous people. Portland stories suggest that conies abandoning the warrens behind Chesil Beach, set up by monks in the twelfth century, were forecasting inundation by the sea – until recently a terrifying prospect for Chiswell. Preferred terms are furry creatures and underground mutton (fear does not extend to eating them: a butcher from Fortuneswell started the Portland Ra**it Club during the Second World War). Since the islanders do so much quarrying, another explanation hinges on animals portending danger of rockfalls.

But fishermen in Craster and some families in other Northumbrian villages have the same problem. Is this an ancient prejudice – fear and superstition carried coastwise from far away? Katrina Porteous, working as a visiting poet on Shetland, found the same avoidance, and Robert Graves mentioned the fisher folk of the Scottish islands steering clear of the word. He pointed out that the two sacred and tabooed beasts mentioned in Leviticus and native here are the hare and the pig.

Although the hare may be indigenous and carries with it much folklore and superstition, the ra**it was brought here by the Romans. Around Flamborough in Yorkshire mention of either word would have put paid to the day's fishing in the nineteenth century.

Across Europe the word p*g carries much ill luck; anciently it was held to presage thunder, lightning and big winds. One can understand, then, how mention of its name at sea would be an ill omen. In the North East alternative names include grunt, article, minister, gadgy ('old man', Holy Island), John Alec (Seahouses), guffy or grice (Beadnell) and gissie (Newcastle). Ra**its, too, are avoided in Beadnell, where they are called caldies.

Fishing, quarrying and mining demand that men (women are unlucky, too) risk their lives every day in ways most of us cannot imagine, providing good reason to be alert, to have fears. These are among the oldest of activities – do they also share some history, trading culture across land and sea?

WAREHOUSES

Mills, factories and warehouses were buildings of stature in the eighteenth and nineteenth centuries. They are increasingly finding favour for new uses, being attractive and well built, embedded and understood, as well as embodying local memories. Warehouses keep company with docks, canals and railways and Victorian industrial towns, and are particularly fine in the textile towns of Lancashire and Yorkshire, such as Manchester, Leeds, Bradford, Dewsbury and Batley. Many have been lost to fire, bombed or demolished.

Manchester's imposing brick warehouses were not just store-rooms, but places where buyers came to look at and buy goods. From the 1840s they were often built in a grand style known as Italian palazzo, which was later replicated in other parts of the country. In Yorkshire, Bradford's limestone warehouses served its wool-textile industry. Many were demolished in the 1960s and 1970s, but some survive in Little Germany,

Butlers Wharf, London.

the twenty-acre quarter inhabited by German wool merchants in the nineteenth century, and are undergoing regeneration. The grand façades of Batley, designed to greet buyers, created, as Mark Girouard said, '*a city of palaces even if the palaces have fallen on hard days*'.

Liverpool's docks and warehouses were built to serve its position as a pre-eminent trading city, the tall brick warehouses storing a wide variety of goods, from tea, sugar, spices and rice to silks, cotton, wool and tobacco. The early warehouses were three to six storeys high and built of mud-brown brick, with distinctive, inset central loading doors and overhanging timber hoist beams below the roof. With timber floors and stanchions, many succumbed to fire, so iron began to replace wood in vulnerable places.

Anthony Lyster's fourteen-storey tobacco warehouse on Stanley Dock, built between 1897 and 1901 with hydraulic lifts, was reputed at the

Gloucester docks.

time to be the largest in the world. Also enormous were the bonded fire-proof warehouses built by Jesse Hartley around Albert, Stanley and Wapping Docks. These monuments to trade were recognised with Liverpool's designation as a World Heritage City in 2004, which should help to conserve its industrial heritage and buildings. Many of the surviving 150 or so warehouses need to be refurbished and new uses found for them, without destroying their distinctive characters.

Dutch and Flemish styles are visible in warehouses lining Great Yarmouth's Hall Quay and South Quay in Norfolk, at the confluence of the rivers Yare, Bure and Waveney. In the West Country 'Bristol Byzantine' was coined to describe the north Italian influence on this city's nineteenth-century warehouses. Fifteen tall, yellow-brick warehouses surround the canal basin at Gloucester docks; built to store grain and iron, they are now being redeveloped into antiques emporia, apartments, cafés and shops.

The Thames and the London docks were lined with warehouses. They were usually less impressive than in the northern cities, and many were lost to wartime bombing and post-war redevelopment. Narrow lanes that squeeze between tall, utilitarian buildings are typified by Clink Street and Shad Thames in Southwark and by Wapping Wall on the north bank of the river. Elsewhere city enclaves, such as Clerkenwell and Smithfield, notable for their surviving warehouses, are much sought after for the personality that their age, quality and density brings. The area to the north of the Piazza in Covent Garden was full of fruit and vegetable warehouses. Some were demolished, but, following enormous local and national effort, much of the area was saved from comprehensive redevelopment in the 1970s. In all these examples the buildings and narrow streets have proved adaptable for large and small lofts, flats, studios, offices, galleries, cafés and shops. Many still flaunt their original names, owners or functions.

WHALES, DOLPHINS & PORPOISES

In March 2004 a fifteen-ton sperm whale was stranded in shallow waters off the Wash, proving that large whales are not confined to far-flung places – some feed off our shores and pass through on migration from feeding to breeding grounds. But there is more chance of spotting some of the smaller cetaceans, including dolphins and porpoises. Of the 28 species that have been recorded in our territorial waters, ten are annual visitors or residents, including the common, bottlenose, Risso's and white-beaked dolphins, harbour porpoise and minke whale.

We have changed from being a whaling nation to a whale-watching one. Whaling was encouraged by the British government with bounty incentives, and the main whaling ports of Hull and Whitby in Yorkshire, Newcastle upon Tyne, Liverpool and London prospered from the Greenland whale fishery. By 1818, 64 ships were sailing from Hull, and two years later 688 whales were caught, producing eight thousand tons of whalebone. From here and the whaling stations established on the island of South Georgia, according to Friends of the Earth, '*Britain helped to kill off the Blue Whales of the Antarctic and North Atlantic and the North Atlantic Right Whale*'.

Popular opinion has become increasingly appalled at our treatment of these intelligent mammals. In 1972 the British government signed a United Nations resolution for a ten-year moratorium on all commercial whaling, but it was not imposed by the International Whaling Commission until the 1985/6 season. It continues to be extended, despite opposition from Japan, Norway and Iceland.

Now whales and dolphins are protected in British territorial waters. It seems ironic that as we have discovered an affection for our coastal cetaceans they are rapidly being killed by fishing fleets. Hundreds of dolphins are inadvertently caught in the nets of pair-trawlers (nets as large as two football pitches dragged between two boats) and are found washed up on the beaches of Devon and Cornwall. Discerning restaurants refuse to cook with bass caught by pair-trawlers. UK boats are banned from pair-trawling within twelve miles of the coast in our territorial waters, but not within our two-hundred-mile offshore area, which includes the continental shelf.

Harbour porpoises appear to be declining in number, no doubt for the same reason, especially in the southern North Sea and English Channel. But they can be seen off the coast of Northumberland and from Flamborough Head and Spurn Head in Yorkshire from July to September.

Today bottlenose dolphins are the species most frequently seen in small groups off the Northumberland coast in summer, especially around the Farne Islands. They sometimes venture up east-coast estuaries, such as the Blackwater, Crouch and Thames, and are spotted from south, south-west and north-west coasts in summer.

The common dolphin enjoys bow-riding with boats off the south-west coast, and Risso's dolphin might take a look at you if you are on the ferry between Portsmouth and Bilbao, Spain in winter or sailing off the west coasts between May and September. During 2004 Risso's were seen in unprecedented numbers in the North Sea, thought to be following squid northwards as waters grow warmer. Killer whales (orcas) have been seen off Cornwall and the Isles of Scilly during May.

The sighting of a whale was always a big occasion. In his diary John Evelyn wrote of a 58-foot baleen whale in the river Thames: '*A large whale was taken betwixt my land abutting on the Thames and Greenwich, which drew an infinite concourse to see it, by water, horse, coach, and on foot, from London, and all parts.*' Nevertheless it was killed with a 'harping iron'. We have different sensibilities now. In January 2006, thousands of Londoners watched an eighteen-foot northern bottlenose whale that had strayed far from her Atlantic Ocean feeding grounds make her way slowly up the Thames to Battersea Bridge, and were saddened by her death as rescuers tried to move her to deeper waters.

The closest that most of us will get to a whale is in the Oxford University Museum of Natural History or the Natural History Museum in London. The life-sized model of a blue whale never fails to amaze. The last dolphinarium closed in 1993, opinion popularly agreeing that confinement for these creatures has no place in a civilised society.

WHITE CLIFFS

The whiteness of our southern cliffs may be the source of the ancient name Albion. The whiteness is chalk – pure, lime-rich rock made up of billions upon billions of '*coccoliths secreted by algae*' (Richard Fortey). The White Cliffs of Dover are emblems of England.

> *... on the French coast the light*
> *Gleams and is gone; the cliffs of England stand,*
> *Glimmering and vast, out in the tranquil bay.*
>
> MATTHEW ARNOLD, from 'Dover Beach'

Developments and sea defences now protect the base of the cliffs, so rockfalls are less common and this stretch of cliffs is green with growth.

In *King Lear* (Act IV, scene vi) Edgar's description of what is now called Shakespeare Cliff in Kent captures the scale and power:

> *How fearful*
> *And dizzy 'tis to cast one's eyes so low!*
> *The crows and choughs that wing the mid-way air*
> *Show scarce so gross as beetles. Half-way down*
> *Hangs one that gathers samphire – dreadful trade!*
> *Methinks he seems no bigger than his head.*
> *The fishermen that walk upon the beach*
> *Appear like mice.*

Hunstanton, Norfolk.

Flamborough Head, Yorkshire.

Often soft enough to bite and chew to assuage your indigestion, chalk is structurally capable of standing up to the elements. It can form the highest of cliffs: at Beachy Head and the Seven Sisters in Sussex the cliffs reach more than five hundred feet and they are topped by some of the richest chalk grassland. Continual undercutting by the sea causes constant rockfalls, which keeps these bastions glistening white and beautiful.

England has almost sixty per cent of the chalk coast of Europe and many of its best habitats. Its softness supports shells and sponges that bore, as well as green seaweeds, all peculiar to the chalk.

Great sweeping cliffs along the Dorset coast are edged by golden sand, with Durdle Door and Bat's Head demonstrating the formation of arches. The contortions of the chalk, so folded as the Alps were rising, are apparent in the thin line of chalk that makes spectacular sea stacks: Old Harry and his Wife on the Purbeck side and the Needles by the Isle of Wight. At Freshwater Bay, Isle of Wight the lines of flints show the chalk has been turned almost vertical from its horizontal bedding.

As far west as Devon at Beer Head the chalk appears again, high, proud and slightly green; around the corner landslips contort the Hooken Cliffs, but pinnacles of chalk peer out to sea.

In Norfolk a surprise awaits: the sixty-foot cliffs at Hunstanton are of red chalk, full of iron compounds, topped with white chalk.

The great north-facing cliffs at Speeton and Bempton in Yorkshire, with the cliffs and promontory of Flamborough Head, are different again: calcium carbonate has fortified the chalk, giving it greater resistance and a sugary look. But the weaknesses are relentlessly sought out by the sea, as witnessed by the deep coves, arches, stacks and caves. On the shore there are seaweeds and invertebrates found nowhere else in England. Bempton Cliffs reach four hundred feet, and among the 33 species of seabird, vulnerable now to the changing fortunes of the North Sea, are gannets, guillemots, kittiwakes and puffins (known locally as mackerel gant, scout, petrel and Flamborough Head pilot), which gather in unparalleled colonies here from April to mid-August.

WINDS

The wind tantalises us with its invisible power – in many cultures this is the breath of god, the founding mystery. It is a source of violence, gentleness and miracles.

East Anglia and the South suffer between twenty and sixty tornadoes a year. The Parish Map of Selsey in Sussex shows a little whirlwind gathering in the sea, dated 1998. This stretch of country seems to attract spirals of wind that can do significant damage to roofs and trees.

On 8 December 1954 a tornado streaked from Chiswick to Southgate – nine miles – across London at 212 miles per hour, devastating a strip up to four hundred yards wide. People saw cars lifted fifteen feet in the air. When a tornado that was centred on Small Heath, Birmingham took the roofs off tens of houses and uprooted hundreds of trees on 28 July 2005, someone reported seeing a lucky ten-year-old boy fly through the air, as though playing Quidditch, and land back on the ground.

Wind is measured on the Beaufort scale. It runs from Force 0, with a wind speed of less than one mile per hour, through Gale Force 8 (30–35mph) to Hurricane Force 12 (60–100mph). Hearing Storm Force 11 carefully spelled out on the Shipping Forecast is not unusual and, rarely, hurricanes come this way. Camden told how Albion was surrounded by terrible northern winds and unpassable seas and that '*some are for placing the nativity of the winds here-abouts, as if they had been all generated here, and the confluence of matter had made this island its general rendezvous*'. Certainly history tells stories of Julius Caesar, the Spanish Armada and other miscreants being scattered by the winds – it seems they have sometimes served us well.

On fine days the coast also enjoys sea breezes, which flow inland from a cool sea to hotter land when opposite winds are not too strong. At night this situation is reversed, giving rise to an offshore 'land breeze'. Fishermen know and use these well. On the peninsula of Devon and Cornwall sea breezes from north and south converge, producing eastward-marching bands of cumulus cloud; glider pilots learn to beware of the 'sea breeze bottleneck', where the land narrows north of Lyme Bay, which must be crossed during flights to the west. East Anglian farmers south of the Wash curse the sea breeze when it blows in bean aphids or contaminating pollen from wild sugar beet near the coast.

It is from the west that our prevailing winds help the Gulf Stream to keep us warmer than our latitude would suggest. They bring rain and are lured to drop it by westerly hills and the Pennines. Shelley's 'Ode to the West Wind' opines: '*Wild Spirit, which art moving everywhere;/Destroyer and Preserver; hear, O hear!*' He ends with the optimistic lines: '*if Winter comes, can Spring be far behind?*' It is the north wind that brings us winter, and the east wind that consolidates it, blowing from the 'wastes of Siberia'. In summer an easterly wind brings the heat and dryness of the great continental landmass. Winds from the south help our winged migrants to reach us – red admirals, swallows – flying from Africa via Europe. The south wind also brings occasional 'blood rains', sand carried from the Sahara high in the atmosphere for 1,600 miles. On 1 July 1968 people all the way from Liphook in Hampshire to the Midlands had to clear layers of red dust from their cars and homes after a dry wind.

Most cultures have names for particular winds. We have but one: the feared easterly Helm Wind, which blows down into Cumberland from the Pennines. It is astonishingly local, blasting the villages that lie in the shadow of the Cross Fell range in the Eden valley – Gamblesby, Kirkland, Melmerby, Milburn and Ousby – but said never to cross the Eden. Whenever the wind blows, telltale cloud formations appear, known as the Helm Cloud and the Helm Bar. Locals dread its onset in spring and autumn, for it can roar like a train for days on end when the conditions are right. It scorches vegetation, knocks sheep and people off their feet, rips slates from roofs, even makes farm gates impossible to open. John Ruskin regarded it as one of the '*Plague Winds*' of the world. Gail Vines explains what Gordon Manley, a twentieth-century geographer, discovered: '*The secret of the helm wind lies in the unique ramp-shape of the Pennine Ridge: a gentle upward sloping approach on the east, a solid, unbroken ridge crest and a steep but very long, smooth descent on the western, lee side. Once air has passed over the ridge, it becomes warmer, drier and faster. With no obstacles to slow its progress on the downward slope, the wind acquires tremendous force.*'

Other places have a reputation: Windwhistle Hill, near Chard in Somerset, Windhill in west Yorkshire and Windle in Lancashire are all

Hawthorn.

descriptive names. The tower of St Botolph's, or the Boston Stump, in Lincolnshire attracts the breezes; it is said that the piety of the prospective saint so disturbed the devil that he huffed and puffed strongly enough that the wind never leaves. A strong gust of wind in Cheshire might be called Whittle, following a grisly incident in the wind in the sixteenth century, involving a dropped coffin bearing a Captain of the same name. A puff of wind in Cornwall may get noted as a waddy. Meg Amsden reports that in the Norfolk/Suffolk Broads sudden winds are known as Rogers – they have been known to drive boats up the banks and to strip windmills of their sails.

The people who gather on Parliament Hill in north London to fly their kites, and participants in Kite Festivals, for example on Barbury Castle near Swindon, Wiltshire, make visible the unseeable. So do the billowing sails of the dinghies on Hornsea Mere in Yorkshire and the wind surfers' movements in Chichester and Langstone harbours in Hampshire. The sport was invented by Peter Chilvers off Hayling Island in the late 1950s.

Even though you cannot see the wind, the sheltering sycamores around Pennine farms, the sculpted forms of the beeches across Exmoor in Devon, the shapes and orientations of harbours, the floating presence of the buzzard and the flight path of planes landing at Manchester airport all tell of its dominance and direction.

ZAWNS

The coast of Cornwall is intricately carved by the waves. Its hard rocks notwithstanding, many narrow clefts have been etched by the sea; in the west Cornish dialect these are called zawns. Softer minerals in the Permian granite, including tin and also copper – staining the rocks with bright verdigris (turret-roof green) – have succumbed to marine erosion along the veins, often leaving vertical cliffs on all sides. Sometimes these have been further accentuated by mining.

Zawn a Bal means mine cleft. At Barrett's Zawn a tunnel, now fallen in, was made to move slate to the sea. Botallack Loe Warren Zawn offers more than 23 minerals, including copper, cuprite and malachite and also botallackite. Nearby Stamps and Jowl Zawn offers twelve minerals (the misheard *stampez an jowl* means the devil's stamping mill). Zawn Buzz and Gen is the English attempt to make sense of *bos an gean* – the giant's home. Only too often language and dialect are flattened by surveyors.

Chough Zawn embodies both avian history and hope. This proud, black, red-billed bird is the emblem of Cornwall; perhaps its aerial acrobatics will once more be seen here. Climbers love these challenging cliff faces. Great Zawn offers magnificent granite climbing, exposed to the westerly elements and above the ocean swells, with 220 feet of multi-pitch routes, including Desolation Row, Xanadu, Dream and Liberator.

On the granite Isle of Lundy Big Zawn, Grand Falls Zawn and Arch Zawn are known as good climbs. In Wales and on the Isle of Portland in Dorset the word re-emerges; in Breton the word *saon* means valley. Back in Penwith, Cornwall a walk around the coastal path will introduce you to at least 35 zawns in the granite between Newlyn and St Ives.

Short Bibliography & References

See *England in Particular* for fuller Bibliography

Introduction
Clifford, Sue and King, Angela (Eds). *Local Distinctiveness: Place Particularity and Identity*. Conference Papers. Common Ground, 1993.

Albion
Ackroyd, Peter. *Albion*. Chatto and Windus, 2002.

Collins, Roger and McClure, Judith (Eds). *Bede The Ecclesiastical History of the English People*. OUP, 1969/1994.

Evans, Ivor H (revised by). *Brewer's Dictionary of Phrase and Fable*. Cassell, 1990.

Westwood, Jennifer. *Albion*. Paladin, 1987.

Alexanders
Mabey, R. *Flora Britannica*. Chatto and Windus, 1996.

Vickery, A. *A Dictionary of Plant Lore*. OUP, 1995.

Ammonites
Bassett, Michael G. *'Formed Stones', Folklore and Fossils*. National Museum of Wales, 1982.

British Mesozoic Fossils. British Museum (Natural History), 1967.

Arches
Steers, J.A. *The Coastline of England and Wales*. CUP, 1964.

Artists' Colonies & Schools
Jacobs, M. and Warner, M. *The Phaidon Companion to Art and Artists in the British Isles*. Phaidon, 1980.

Bandstands
Girouard, Mark. *The English Town*. Yale University Press, 1990.

Weir, Christopher. *Village and Town Bands*. Shire, 1981.

Basking Sharks
'Fish of the day'. *BBC Wildlife Magazine*, May 2004.

Beaches
Hudston, S. *Islomania*. Agre, 2000.

The Good Beach Guide. Marine Conservation Society.

Beach Huts
Ferry, Kathryn. *Sheds on the Seashore: A Tour Through Beach Hut History*. Indepenpress Publishing Ltd, 2009.

Gershlick, Janet. *Southwold Beach Huts*. Hair-Raising Publications, 2003.

Beacons (Coastal)
Somerville, Christopher. *English Harbours and Coastal Villages*. Weidenfeld and Nicolson, 1989.

Blackpool Rock
Race, Margaret. *The Story of Blackpool Rock*. 1990.

Blow Holes
Robinson, Adrian and Millward, Roy. *The Shell Book of the British Coast*. David and Charles, 1983.

Boats
Elmer, W. *The Terminology of Fishing: A Survey of English and Welsh Inshore Fishing Things and Words*. The Cooper Monographs, 19 English Dialect Series. Franke Verlag, 1973.

McKee, Eric. *Working Boats of Britain: their shape and purpose*. Conway Maritime Press, 1983.

Porteous, K. (Ed). *The Bonny Fisher Lad: Memories of the North Northumberland Fishing Community*. The People's History, 2003.

Williamson, T. *The Norfolk Broads: A Landscape History*. Manchester University Press, 1997.

Bores

Hole, Christina. *English Folklore*. Batsford, 1940.

Witts, C. *The Mighty Severn Bore*. River Severn Publications, 1999.

The Severn Bore and Trent Aegir Predictions. Environment Agency, 2003,4,5.

The Channel

Bonavia, Michael. *The Channel Tunnel Story*. David and Charles, 1987.

Mortimore, Rory. *The Chalk of Sussex and Kent*. The Geologist's Association, 1997.

Smith, Hillas. *The English Channel*. Images Publishing, 1994.

Chines

Priest, Becky. *Island Chines*. Isle of Wight Council, 1998.

The Chines of Bournemouth and Poole. Bournemouth Borough Council, nd.

Choughs

Buczacki, Stefan. *Fauna Britannica*. Hamlyn, 2002.

Wingfield Gibbons, David et al. *The New Atlas of Breeding Birds in Britain and Ireland 1988-1991*. BTO, 1993.

Cliffs

Ratcliffe, D.A (Ed). *A Nature Conservation Review*. CUP, 1977.

Steers, J.A. *The Coastline of England and Wales*. CUP, 1964.

Birds, Summer 2000.

Coastline

Fortey, Richard. *The Hidden Landscape* Jonathan Cape, 1993.

Porteous, Katrina. *Turning the Tide* (Pattison, Keith; Porteous, Katrina; Soden, Robert). District of Easington, 2001.

Raban, Jonathan. *Coasting*. Collins Harvill, 1986.

Coasts

Covey, R. and Laffoley, D.d'A. *State of Nature: Maritime - getting onto an even keel*. English Nature, 2002.

Soothill, Eric and Thomas, Michael. *The Natural History of Britain's Coasts*. Blandford Publishing, 1987.

Living with the Sea. English Nature, 2003.

Cobles

Porteous, K (Ed). *The Bonny Fisher Lad*. The People's History, 2003.

Cornish Gigs

McKee, Eric. *Working Boats of Britain: their shape and purpose*. Conway Maritime Press, 1983.

Counties

Davies, N. *The Isles: a History*. Papermac, 2000.

Denton, P. (Ed). *Betjeman's London*. John Murray, 1988.

Association of British Counties website: www.abcounties.co.uk

Coves

Blyton, Enid. *Five on a Treasure Island*. Hodder and Stoughton, 1942.

Perkins, J.W. *Geology Explained in Dorset*. David and Charles, 1977.

Deezes

Peak, Steve (Ed). *Hastings Stade, The Fishing Beach and Maritime History*. Hastings Borough Council, 1995.

Estuaries

Rothschild, Miriam and Marren, Peter. *Rothschild's Reserves*. Harley Books, 1997.

Soper, Tony. *A Natural History Guide to the Coasts*. Webb and Bower/National Trust, 1984.

Living with the Sea. English Nature, 2003.

Fish & Chips

Ellis, Hattie. *Eating England*. Mitchell Beazley, 2001.

Harben, Philip. *Traditional Dishes of Britain*. Bodley Head, 1953.

Fog & Mist

Hague, D.B. and Christie, R. *Lighthouses: their Architecture, History and Archaeology*. Gomer Press, 1975.

Westwood, Jennifer. *Albion*. Paladin, 1987.

Frets

Houghton, D. *Weather at Sea*. Fernhurst Books, 1998.

'Staithes Song'. Composed by Staithes villagers with Blaize.

Funicular Railways

Body, Geoffrey and Eastleigh, Robert L. *Cliff Railways of the British Isles*. David and Charles, 1964.

Lindley, Kenneth. *Seaside Architecture*. Hugh Evelyn, 1973.

Ganseys

Thompson, Gladys. *Guernsey and Jersey Patterns*. Batsford, 1955.

North East Fisher Gansies. Tyne and Wear County Council Museums, 1980.

Grazing Marshes

Chris Blandford Associates. *The Solway Coast Landscape*. Countryside Commission, 1995.

UK Biodiversity, priority habitats: coastal and floodplain grazing marsh. JNCC, 2001.

Harbours

Adlard Coles, K. *The Shell Pilot to the English Channel*. Faber and Faber, 1985.

Williamson, J.A. *The English Channel*. Collins, 1959.

Hards

Kim Wilkie Environmental Design. *Thames Landscape Strategy: Hampton to Kew*. Thames Landscape Steering Group, 1994.

Public Launch Points on the Hampshire Coast – a position paper. Hampshire County Council, 1994.

Islands

Grigson, Geoffrey. *The Scilly Isles*. Duckworth, 1977.

Hudston, Sara. *Islomania*. Agre Books, 2000.

Langham, A.F. *The Island of Lundy*. Alan Sutton, 1994.

Jet

Muller, Helen. *Jet Jewellery and Ornaments*. Shire, 2003.

Kippers

Grigson, Jane. *Good Things*. Penguin Books, 1973.

Mason, Laura with Brown, Catherine. *Traditional Foods of Britain*. Prospect, 1999.

Lagoons

Grigson, Geoffrey, *Geoffrey Grigson's Countryside*. Ebury Press, 1982.

Lidos

Powers, Alan (Ed). *Farewell My Lido*. Thirties Society, 1991.

Smith, Janet. *Liquid assets: the lidos and open air swimming pools of Britain*. English Heritage 2005.

Lighthouses

Ashley, Peter. *Guiding Lights*. English Heritage/Everyman, 2001.

Hague, Douglas B. and Christie, Rosemary. *Lighthouses*. Gomer, 1975.

Mason, Benedict. *Lighthouses of England and Wales*. Collins Classics CD, 1991.

Porteous, Katrina. 'Longstone Light' in *The Lost Music*. Bloodaxe Books, 1996.

Woodman , Richard and Wilson, Jane. *The Lighthouses of Trinity House*. Thomas Reed, 2002.

Links

Gates, Phil. 'Home from Home'. *BBC*

Wildlife Magazine, August 2004. English Nature.

Lost Villages

O'Riordan, Tim. emails, 2005.

Westwood, Jennifer. *Albion: A legendary Guide to Britain*. Paladin, 1985.

Willson, Beccles. *Lost England – the story of our submerged coasts*. George Newnes, 1902.

Wood, Eric S. *Historical Britain*. Harvill Press, 1995.

Martello Towers

Hollands, Ray and Harris, Paul. *Along the Kent Coast*. Sutton Publishing, 2003.

English Heritage.

Natterjack Toads

Bridson, R.H. *The Natterjack Toad*. Nature Conservancy Council, 1978.

Simpson, David. 'The fall and rise of Ainsdale's Natterjacks'. *British Wildlife*, February 2002.

Smith, Philip H. 'The Sefton Coast sand-dunes, Merseyside'. *British Wildlife*, October 2000.

Nobbies

McKee, Eric. *Working Boats of Britain: their shape and purpose*. Conway Maritime Press, 1983.

'Obby 'Osses

Alford, Violet. *The Hobby Horse and other Animal Masks*. The Merlin Press, 1978.

Sykes, Homer. *Once a Year: Some Traditional British Customs*. Gordon Fraser, 1977.

Oysters

Kightly, Charles. *The Customs and Ceremonies of Britain*. Thames and Hudson, 1986.

Trewin, Carol and Woolfitt, Adam. *Gourmet Cornwall*. Alison Hodge, 2005.

Younge, C.M. *Oysters*. Collins, 1960.

Native Oyster (Ostrea edulis) *Biodiversity Action Plan*. English Nature, 1999.

Pantiles

Clifton-Taylor, Alec. *The Pattern of English Building*. Faber and Faber, 1972.

Crowden, James and Rook, Pauline. *Bridgwater: The Parrett's Mouth*. Agre Books, 2000.

Penoyre, John and Penoyre, Jane. *Houses in the Landscape: A Regional Study of Vernacular Building Styles in England and Wales*. Readers Union, 1978.

Penny Hedge

Kightly, Charles. *The Customs and Ceremonies of Britain*. Thames and Hudson, 1986.

Horne's Guide to Whitby and District, c.1975.

Piers

Coombes, Nigel. *Striding Boldly*. Clevedon Pier Trust, 1995.

Mickleborough, Timothy J. *Guide to British Piers*. National Piers Society, 1998.

Pillboxes

Osborne, Mike. *Defending Britain. Twentieth Century Military structures in the Landscape*. Tempus 2004.

English Heritage Conservation Bulletin 44, June 2003.

Portland Lerrets

Elmer, W. *The Terminology of Fishing: A Survey of English and Welsh Inshore Fishing. Things and Words*. The Cooper Monographs, 19 English Dialect Series. Franke Verlag, 1973.

McKee, Eric. *Working Boats of Britain: their shape and purpose*. Conway Maritime Press, 1983.

Punch and Judy

Herbert, Trevor (Ed). *The British Brass Band, A Musical and Social History*. OUP, 2000.

Simpson, J. and Roud, S. *Oxford Dictionary of English Folklore*. OUP, 2000.

Quicksand

Timberlake, R.R. 'Crossing the Sands' in *Keer to Kent, a look at life in the Arnside/ Silverdale Area of Outstanding Natural Beauty from 1986 to 2000* (Ayre, Barry, Ed). Arnside/Silverdale Landscape Trust, 2001.

Rias

Derek Lovejoy Partnership. *The South Devon Landscape*. Countryside Commission, 1993.

Salt Marshes

Chris Blandford Associates. *The Solway Coast Landscape*. Countryside Commission, 1995.

JNCC. *UK Biodiversity Priority Habitats: coastal salt marsh*. 2001.

Sand-Dunes

Pye, K. and French, P.W. *Targets for coastal habitat re-creation*. English Nature, 1993.

Tansley, A.G. *Britain's Green Mantle*. George Allen and Unwin, 1968.

Sea Caves

Perkins, J.W. *Geology explained in Dorset*. David and Charles, 1977.

Kent Underground.

Sea Fish

Duncan, Katherine. *An Introduction to England's Marine Wildlife*. English Nature, 1992.

Starkey, Ed D; Reid, C; Ashcroft, N. *England's Sea Fisheries*. Chatham Publishing, 2000.

Field Guide to the Water Life of Britain. Reader's Digest, 1984.

Sea Forts

Turner, Stephen. Emails, 2004 and 2005. Project Redsand.

Sea-Marks

Aylard Coles, K. *The Shell Pilot to the South Coast Harbours*. Faber and Faber, 1939.

Legg, Rodney. *Durdle Door and White Nothe, Purbeck Coastal Walks*. Dorset Publishing Company, 1995.

Sea Tractor

Barber, Chips. *Around and About Burgh Island and Bigbury on Sea*. Obelisk Publications, 1998.

Shellfish

Mason, Laura with Brown, Catherine. *Traditional Foods of Britain*. Prospect Books, 1999.

Stein, Rick. *Seafood Lovers' Guide*. BBC Worldwide, 2000.

Shingle

Robinson, Ged. *Dungeness: a unique place*. Sutton House, 1988.

Rothschild, Miriam and Marren, Peter. *Rothschild's Reserves: Time and fragile nature*. Balaban Publishers and Harley Books, 1997.

Shipping Forecast

Meteorological Office.

Sound Mirrors

Barrett, Claire. *Sound Mirrors, Greatstone, Kent* The Twentieth Century Society. 2003.

Arts Council.

English Heritage.

Stacks

Steers, J.A. *The Coastline of England and Wales*. CUP, 1964.

Starfish

Barrett, John. *Life on the Seashore*. Collins, 1974.

Elmer, W. *The Terminology of Fishing. A Survey of English and Welsh Inshore Fishing Things and Words*. The Cooper

Monographs 19, English Dialect Series.
Franke Verlag, 1973.

Surfing

Nerlson, Chris and Taylor, Demi. Surfing
Britain (Footprints Surfing Guide).
Footprint Handbooks, 2005.

Thames Sailing Barges

Hazell, Martin. *Sailing Barges*. Shire Album,
2001.

Tide Mills

Southgate, Michael. *The Old Tide Mill at
Eling*. Eling Tide Mill Trust, nd.

Tides

Baber, Tim. *Mudeford Sandbank News*, Late
Summer, 1999.

Graham, Frank. *Holy Island, a short history
guide*. Butler, 1987.

Rose, Lesley. *Treacherous Sands*. British
Video History Trust, 1998.

Unlucky Words

Baker, M. *The Folklore of the Sea*. David and
Charles, 1928/1979.

Fowles, John. *Islands*. Jonathan Cape,
1978.

Graves, Robert. *The White Goddess*. Faber
and Faber, 1961.

Warehouses

Giles, Colum and Hawkins, Bob.
Storehouses of Empire: Liverpool's
Historic Warehouses, English Heritage,
2004.

Girouard, Mark. *The English Town*. Yale
University Press, 1990.

Whales, Dolphins & Porpoises

Hart Davies, Duff. *Fauna Britannica*.
Weidenfeld and Nicolson, 2002.

Macdonald, D.W. and Tattersall, Fran.
*Britain's Mammals: The Challenge for
Conservation*. PTES, 2001.

Whale Campaign Manuals, 1 and 2. Friends of
the Earth, 1972 and 1974.

White Cliffs

Fortey, Richard. *The Hidden Landscape*.
Jonathan Cape, 1993.

Robinson, A and Millward, R. *The Shell Book
of the British Coast*. David and Charles,
1983.

Winds

Defoe, D. 'The Storm 1704' in *Defoe's Works*,
vol v. George Bell and Sons, 1879.

Manley, Gordon. *Climate and the British
Scene*. Collins, 1952.

Simpson, John E. *Sea Breeze and Local Wind*.
CUP, 1994.

The Macmillan Nautical Almanac 1997.
Macmillan, 1996.

Zawns

Arkell, W.J. and Tomkeieff, S.I. *English Rock
Terms*. OUP, 1953.

Whittaker, David. *Zawn Lens*. Wavestone
Press, 2003.

The Illustrators:

Richard Allen, *Albion*, page 1; *Coasts*, page 37; *Islands*, page 63; *White Cliffs*, page 124

Brian Grimwood, *Ammonites*, page 3

Angela Hogg, *Arches*, page 6, 7; *Deezes*, page 46; *Ganseys*, page 56; *Lighthouses*, page 68; *Punch and Judy*, page 88

Sue Williams, *Artists' Colonies & Schools*, page 9

Ivan Allen, *Bandstands*, page 11; *Beach Huts*, page 16, 17; *Coastguard Cottages*, page 32; *Funicular Railways*, page 54; *Pillboxes*, page 86; *Sea Tractor*, page 100; *Stacks*, page 109; *Warehouses*, page 118

Grahame Baker Smith, *Beaches*, page 13; *Warehouses*, page 119

Glyn Goodwin, *Beacons (coastal)*, page 18; *Martello Towers*, page 73; *Sand-Dunes*, page 93 (left)

Mary Roberts-Hogan, *Blackpool Rock*, page 20

Clifford Harper, *Bores*, page 23

Lucinda Rogers, *Chines*, page 27

David Holmes, *Choughs*, page 28; *Coastline*, page 34

Katrina Porteous, *Cobles*, page 39

David Atkinson, *Counties*, page 43; *Harbours*, page 59; *Sand-Dunes*, page 93 (right); *Shingle*, page 103; *Shipping Forecast*, page 105, 106; *The Channel*, page 25

Dan Williams, *Estuaries*, page 48

John Hinchcliffe, *Fish & Chips*, page 50

Francis Mosley, *Natterjack Toads*, page 74

Ed Briant, *'Obby 'Osses*, page 75, 77

Ken Cox, *Piers*, page 83, 84

Eric McKee, *Portland Lerrets*, page 87

Peter Till, *Rias*, page 90

Ian Beck, *Sea Forts*, page 98; *Sound Mirrors*, page 108

Chloë Cheese, *Shellfish*, page 102

Mick Brownfield, *Starfish*, page 110, 111

Nick Hardcastle, *Tide Mills*, page 113

David Nash, *Winds*, page 127

Selected quotes by permission of:

Hodder & Stoughton Ltd., for *First and Last Loves*, 1952; Caroline Grigson, Literary Executor of the estate of the late Geoffrey Grigson; Sophie Grigson, Literary Executor of the estate of the late Jane Grigson; Readers Union for John and Jane Penoyre, *Houses in the Landscape: a Regional Study of Vernacular Building Styles in England and Wales*, 1978.

Our sincere apologies if we have missed or misrepresented anyone. Please inform us so that we can rectify this.

Acknowledgements

Very many thanks to everyone who contacted us with information about their locality and passions as well as individuals, groups, societies, organisations, publishers, agents, executors and trustees for their generosity. A comprehensive list of thanks and credits is to be found in the full Bibliography and Acknowledgements in *England in Particular*.

Common Ground is a small charity dependent upon grants and donations. We offer most grateful thanks to our funders 1985–2006 including Defra Environmental Action Fund, Carnegie UK Trust, Cobb Trust, John Ellerman Foundation, Garfield Weston Foundation, Headley Trust, Lyndhurst Settlement, Raphael Trust, Tedworth Trust, Countryside Agency, English Nature, National Lottery Arts Council of England, Esmée Fairbairn Charitable Trust, and many more.

Particular thanks to Darren Giddings, Kate O'Farrell, Gail Vines, who helped us research and draft the book and to Katrina Porteous, our Northumberland and literature correspondent; David Holmes, Toby and Polly who oversaw all of the illustrative work; all of the illustrators who responded to our demands for particularity; our trustees and friends: Barbara Bender, Roger Deakin, Robin Grove-White, Richard Mabey, Rupert Nabarro, Fraser Harrison, Robert Hutchison; our agent Vivien Green at Shiel Land; our original mentors at Hodder & Stoughton: Richard Atkinson (especially), Elizabeth Hallett, Nicola Docherty, Simon Shelmerdine, Karen Geary, Rachael Oakden, Hilary Bird, Barbara Roby; designers Stuart Smith, Karl Shanahan, Victoria Forrest.

And in 2013/14 – at John Murray Press Nick Davies MD; at Saltyard Books warm thanks to Elizabeth Hallett – publisher, Kate Miles, Christine Gilland, Lyndsey Ng; designer Clare Skeats and cover illustrator Joe McLaren.

England in Particular was first published in Great Britain in 2006 by Hodder & Stoughton

Journeys Through England in Particular: Coasting was first published in Great Britain in 2014 by Saltyard Books
An imprint of Hodder & Stoughton
An Hachette UK company

Common Ground is a charity (no.326335) and has been grateful for grant support from the Cobb Trust, Countryside Agency, Defra Environmental Action Fund, the John Ellerman Foundation, the Garfield Weston Foundation, the Headley Trust, the Tedworth Charitable Trust, the Lyndhurst Settlement, and many others.

1

Copyright © Sue Clifford and Angela King 2014

The rights of Sue Clifford and Angela King to be identified as the Authors of the Work have been asserted by them in accordance with the Copyright, Designs and Patents Act 1988.

All rights reserved. No part of this publication may be reproduced, stored in a retrieval system, or transmitted, in any form or by any means without the prior written permission of the publisher, nor be otherwise circulated in any form of binding or cover other than that in which it is published and without a similar condition being imposed on the subsequent purchaser.

A CIP catalogue record for this title is available from the British Library.

ISBN 978 1 444 78963 8
eBook ISBN 978 1 444 78964 5

Book design by Clare Skeats
Typeset in Portrait Text and Gill Sans

Printed and bound in China by C&C Offset Printing Co., Ltd

Hodder & Stoughton policy is to use papers that are natural, renewable and recyclable products and made from wood grown in sustainable forests. The logging and manufacturing processes are expected to conform to the environmental regulations of the country of origin.

Saltyard Books
338 Euston Road
London NW1 3BH

www.saltyardbooks.co.uk

BRING THE
COUNTRYSIDE
to the
TOWN.
Keep the fruit, vegetable
and local produce
markets open and alive.
We should be able to buy
NORFOLK BIFFINS
in Norwich and
LAXTON'S SUPERB
in Bedford.

PLACES CARRY
MEANING
in their associations
and symbolisms.
*Don't plough through
significance, it cannot
be re-created.*
The well or tree may be
the reason why a place
is where it is.

LET **NATURE**
IN.
Encourage the plants
that want to grow in
your locality. You'll find
a succession of
GOOD *and* DIVERSE
neighbours that bring
RICHNESS TO
YOUR DOORSTEP.

NAMES CARRY
RESONANCES
AND SECRETS.
RESPECT
LOCAL NAMES
and add new ones with
CARE.
It is not good enough
to call a new estate
'Badger's Mead' when
the badgers have been
DESTROYED.

CHAMPION
THE
ORDINARY
and the
EVERYDAY.

GET TO
KNOW
YOUR PLACE
INTIMATELY.
Search out
PARTICULARITY
AND **PATINA**,
add new
LAYERS
OF
INTEREST.

QUALITY
CANNOT BE
QUANTIFIED.
You know when
something is important
to you – make
SUBJECTIVE
AND *EMOTIONAL*
ARGUMENTS.
Don't be put off because
professionals have
marginalised all the
things they can't count.
MAKE THEM
LISTEN *and* LOOK.

Remember the depth of
PEOPLE'S
ATTACHMENT
TO
PLACES.
Do not undermine
LOCAL PRIDE
and rootedness with
insensitive change.

REVEAL THE
GEOLOGY.
Use the brick and
stone of the locality.
*Reinforce the colour,
patterns, texture,*
CRAFTSMANSHIP
and work of the place.